WHAT OTHERS ARE SAYING ABOUT
When Life Throws You Curves,
Keep Swinging

"*When Life Throws You Curves, Keep Swinging* is an inspirational story about overcoming hardship, living life to the fullest and motivating young men and women to achieve their full potential in baseball and in life. I recommend it for anyone looking to break through life's obstacles and achieve their full potential."
— **Mike Martin, Head Baseball Coach**
Florida State University

"Being a football coach I can certainly understand the difficulties an individual has in motivating their team to do the very best at all times. It is even more difficult when you are an above knee double amputee. Consequently, I found David Vince's book to be inspiring, informative, and a great read."
— **Lou Holtz, ESPN Analyst**

"David Vince has shown courage and perseverance as he overcame the challenges he has faced. We all face difficult situations in life, and through Christ, we can do all things. Submitting to His Spirit is a moment by moment action that He gives us strength to do."
— **Josh Hamilton, Texas Rangers**

"While David has helped develop the careers of a number of players who have gone on to the college and professional ranks, it's impossible to measure the impact he's had on the lives of all the kids he's coached. After playing for him, how could you not be a better person? His story makes competing in the American League East seem like a walk in the park."
— **˙˙˙ddon, Tampa Bay Rays Manager;**
˙ajor League Manager of the Year

"This is a truly inspiring story about a man who has defined the meaning of overcoming adversity. As coaches, we are constantly preaching the importance of perseverance and the ability to prevail over enormous challenges. I believe David Vince personifies these imperative messages in his book, *When Life Throws You Curves, Keep Swinging*. This is a wonderful story of a man who saw challenges as opportunities. Along the way he has inspired everyone with whom he has come into contact. Really amazing story about an amazing man!"

— Paul Mainieri, Head Baseball Coach
Louisiana State University

"David, it was such a pleasure meeting you and I applaud you for your wonderful attitude and for what you have done with your life. You are the epitome of not giving up, and your book should be read by anyone who is going through tough times.

You have proven clearly that adversity only visits the strong but stays forever with the weak and you have chosen to be strong. I deeply admire you and you are a 'blue chipper.' God bless and continue to guide you."

— Dale Brown,
Retired LSU Head Basketball Coach

"Everybody has a curve ball thrown at them during their lifetime. If you haven't had a problem in the past or having one now, you better hang onto your hat because one is coming. Dave faces a handicap not many Americans have faced. However, with his optimistic and joyful demeanor, he still reached the top of the ladder. Read this book and be better prepared for what you will face in life."

— Bobby Bowden,
Legendary College Football Coach

"Indeed, you should keep swinging for the fences. David has a very inspirational book that made me so proud of his tenacity and love for baseball. I hope his story will light a fire for anyone with or without a disability to work hard and earn their dream. Hard work and perseverance will bring success. Don't sit on the bench and wait for things to come your way. Catch Every Ball."

— Johnny Bench,
Baseball Hall of Fame Catcher

WHEN LIFE THROWS YOU CURVES, KEEP SWINGING

WHEN LIFE THROWS YOU CURVES, KEEP SWINGING

A Memoir by
Coach David Vince

with Jeremy M. Harper

LANGMARC
PUBLISHING

AUSTIN, TEXAS

WHEN LIFE THROWS YOU CURVES, KEEP SWINGING
A Memoir by
Coach David Vince
With Jeremy M. Harper

Cover Design: Michael Qualben

Copyright @ 2012 by David Vince
First Printing 2012
Printed in the United States of America
Cover picture permission granted by Ken Clawson
for Clearwater High School Batter-Up Booster Club

Published by
LANGMARC PUBLISHING
P.O. Box 90488
Austin, Texas 78709-0488
www.langmarc.com

Library of Congress Control Number: 2012936889
ISBN: 1-880292-45-9 / 1-978-1-880292-45-7

DEDICATION

To all those who have been told they couldn't achieve their dream ...

To my wife, Susan —
> Thank you for all the sacrifices you have made so that I could follow my dream of a baseball coaching career.

To my Mom, Dad, grandparents, brother, and sister —
> Thank you for believing in me and never letting me say the word "can't" without first having "tried."

To my children —
> May this book inspire you to never quit chasing your dreams no matter what obstacles you may face and to always trust God to fight your battles for you.

To those principals and athletic directors who employed me —
> Thank you for taking the risk of hiring a double amputee baseball coach/teacher, for I never would have realized my dream were it not for you.

CONTENTS

INTRODUCTION

The road to success is not straight. There is a curb called Failure, a loop called Confusion; speed bumps called Friends; red lights called Enemies; caution lights called Family. You will have flats called Jobs, but if you have a spare called Determination, an engine called Perseverance; insurance called Faith, and a driver called Jesus, you will make it to a place called Success!

-Anonymous

In my journey of life and coaching career, I chose the road less traveled. It is certainly an unusual road for a double above-knee amputee since birth, one who never physically played the game of baseball, to pursue a career in athletic coaching. As the passage above indicates, it has not been a path without challenges, obstacles, or setbacks, but is has been a path of opportunity, great accomplishment and reward.

There have been many supportive individuals along my road less traveled journey that offered encouragement, assistance, guidance and direction to enable me to achieve my dream of becoming a successful baseball coach. From principals and athletic directors, who took a chance by hiring a handicapped coach, to assistant coaches and players, who bought into my vision and accepted me, to pastors and youth ministers, who taught me at an early age to have faith and trust God, and loving and supportive parents and grandparents who never allowed me to say can't but always said "you never know till you try."

At an early age I discovered two Bible verses that I adopted as my life verses. Romans 8:28, which said to me God can bring good out of a bad situation. This verse eliminated any self pity early on in my life. The second was Philippians 4:13, which says: "I can do all things through Christ which strengthens me." These verses gave me a strong belief in my own capabilities and the courage to try things others may deem impossible.

The purpose of this book is to encourage others who may be facing difficult or trying times in their lives so that they too can overcome adversity with proper attitude, perspective and determination.

I will share some of the challenges I've faced throughout my life and how overcoming these hardships have strengthened my faith and made me the man I am today. I hope my message inspires, motivates, encourages and uplifts all who read it – just as people before inspired me.

If you take away one thing from reading this book, let it be this: You don't have to be perfect to achieve success, but you do have to be committed.

Chapter 1

Baseball and Bullies

It was August of 1986 in Campbellsville, Kentucky, a small town in central Kentucky about 75 miles south of Louisville. I was 26 and doing what I loved the most: coaching baseball. This was the biggest game of my life up to that point. My team, a small and scrappy group at Campbellsville College, was competing for the Kentucky Intercollegiate Athletic Conference championship. Needing a single win to clinch the title, we found ourselves down 2 to 1 in the bottom half of the final inning. Right fielder Brad Baber was at the plate. Two men were on base. I gave Brad the bunt sign.

It was an improbable position for me to be in. I had just completed my master's degree and a graduate assistantship year at Henderson State in Arkansas, and I was fortunate enough to land the job as the head baseball coach and a physical education instructor at

11

Campbellsville, a small private Southern Baptist NAIA college. After only five years of experience in the coaching ranks (mostly high school), I was a college head coach – only a few years older than some of my players.

My age, though certainly unusual for a college coach, wasn't the most remarkable circumstance of my new vocation. I was born with tibial hemomelia, a congenital bone disease that results in the shortening or a lack of leg bones. Both of my legs were amputated above the knee when I was an infant, and I was fitted with artificial limbs at a very young age. Although I could never play the game, I followed in my father's coaching footsteps and learned to love the game of baseball by watching my younger brother on the field.

I was so grateful that the Athletic Director took a chance on me, the 26-year-old, shaggy-haired double amputee who had never played a single inning of baseball. I was pleasantly surprised how quickly the players accepted me as their coach. Once they realized I knew and loved the game and that I had a vision for the team, they bought in. It was soon full speed ahead.

Still, it wasn't the smoothest start for a college coaching career. I was hired only a week before the fall semester began after the previous coach, Dr. Danny Davis, left over the summer to take another head-coaching gig in North Carolina. I inherited a team of only 21 players, which most notably had only six pitchers on the roster. Very little baseball recruiting had taken place at Campbellsville over the summer because of the coaching vacancy. However, the team wasn't without talent. Campbellsville had finished second in the Kentucky Intercollegiate Athletic Conference four years in a row before my arrival. But with only six pitchers on the roster, I was forced to get creative.

One of my first decisions as coach proved to be an extremely valuable move. In an effort to make my pitching go further, I chopped the regular season schedule by 10 games. Our conference games were 7-inning doubleheaders, so I always made sure I had my best four pitchers ready for each conference doubleheader. My other two pitchers would pitch the midweek games. Predictably, as the season progressed, we found we were winning the conference doubleheaders but losing our midweek games. But overall, the approach worked.

As we approached the final conference double header of the regular season, our overall record was 26-24 with a very good 13-3 conference record. We needed to sweep the last conference doubleheader to take the regular season conference championship. I wanted to win badly. I wanted to reward the administration for taking a chance on me and I wanted my players, who had worked so hard the entire season, to get those conference championship rings.

Our bats came alive in the first game of the doubleheader, and we cruised to a 13 to 1 victory. As is usually the case in baseball, when you experience an offensive flurry in one game, runs are often hard to come by the next time out. That is how we found ourselves down 2-

1 in the bottom of the 7th inning. We had three outs to stage a comeback and clinch the title.

Our first batter up got a base hit, and the next hitter walked, putting runners on first and second with no-body out. Brad Baber stepped to the plate. Brad was a very mature 21-year-old senior who was married, had a baby, was majoring in pre-law, and still playing college baseball at a high level. Brad was a hard-nosed player who put his heart and soul into everything he endeavored.

With our bats cold, I decided we needed to manufacture runs any way we could. I gave Brad the bunt sign to move both our runners into scoring position. Brad squared to bunt and fouled the first pitch off. I gave him another bunt sign. Again, he bunted foul.  With two strikes, I took the bunt sign off and told Brad to swing away, and he didn't disappoint. Brad slammed the very next pitch into the gap for a game winning two-run triple, clinching the first baseball conference championship in Campbellsville College history.

After the game, Brad explained to the local paper: "After screwing up the two bunt attempts, I knew I didn't want to face an upset Coach Vince in the dugout, so I made up my mind to make up for it and I was able to hit the triple in the gap to win the game." Brad Baber was named an Academic All-American after that season and is now a successful lawyer in Indiana.

Our momentum from that come-behind-walk-off win carried us ahead to the final of the regional tournament. We were undefeated, which meant the only way we wouldn't advance to the sectional was if we were beaten twice in a row. But postseason contests were a full nine innings instead of the seven we were accustomed to playing during our conference doubleheaders. Having only six pitchers on our roster finally caught up with us, and we were defeated twice to end our season.

A few days later, I was named KIAC conference coach of the year, which at age 26 was an incredible honor and thrill. I was filled with such a sense of satisfaction that I had proven I was capable of being a successful baseball coach despite being a double amputee. It was one of the highlights of my career.

That success didn't come easy.

***

Eighteen years earlier, as a fourth grader at Northside Elementary in Bogalusa, Louisiana, coaching baseball seemed completely impossible. Surviving the trials and tribulations of grade school as a double amputee was my primary goal. It was September of 1968 early in the school year, and I, like many kids with physical disabilities during that era, was the subject of intense bullying.

I was seven years old and still using wrist crutches to help me walk. There was a small faction of boys who decided they would have some fun at my expense by seeing how many times they could knock me down during recess. Every time the duty teacher turned her back, the boys ran full speed at me, gave me a hard shove, watched me fall and laughed repeatedly. I would pick myself up, dust myself off and a few minutes later they would come again. I told the duty teacher what was going on, but her response was that unless she actually caught them in the act there was nothing she could do. The bullies knew this, so harassing me became an ongoing game for their entertainment.

I endured this daily for about two weeks before I finally got fed up, and I figured out the teacher wasn't going to stop it. I came to the realization that if it were to end, I was the one who was going to have to stop it. On one particular Wednesday lunch recess, I decided to stand up for myself. That day I kept looking over my shoulder anticipating the bully charging me, and like clockwork one boy started approaching at high speed. As the bully closed, I swung my right arm, fully extending my wrist crutch and delivering a direct blow to the bully's stomach so hard it knocked his breath out. The young man, unable to breathe, collapsed like a house of cards and gasped for air. He probably thought he was dying. By the time he finally recovered and started breathing normally again, things had already changed. Because I stood up for myself, the bullies finally left me alone and the recess harassment stopped. The duty teacher never knew what happened.

It wasn't the last time I would be teased. School children can be immature and cruel, particularly when faced with something or someone different from them that they do not understand. Later, my classmates blamed me when we couldn't move to a second-floor classroom (which, believe it or not, in the insulated world of the elementary school student was a big deal) because I couldn't navigate the stairs very efficiently. Although that decision made it easier on me physically, it was emotionally difficult because my classmates blamed me for them not getting the upstairs classroom and saw fit to constantly remind me of this. The bullying came and went but subsided during middle school as the students grew more familiar with my disability and also began to mature.

That experience, and the support of my parents, helped develop a resolve and toughness that I otherwise might not have cultivated. To deal with the stress of harassment and bullying, I developed a mantra of "Vinces are Tough" to help me cope with the bullying. That toughness is something I carried throughout my childhood and into my baseball coaching career. It has served me well in good times and bad. I complimented that toughness with a strong desire to defy expectations.

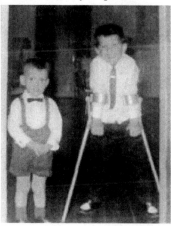

A few months after my incident with my school yard bullies, I would put down my wrist crutches for good. Later that same school year, I was misbehaving at home, as 8-year-olds will do. Mom had had her fill of my bad behavior that day and decided to punish me by taking my crutches away and making me stand in the corner for half an hour. My mom left the room and went about her daily business maintaining our home. When she returned, I had moved from the corner to the far side of the room. Confused, she quizzed me on how I managed to make it to the other side of the room without my crutches. My response was simple. "I walked," I said.

Of course, she couldn't believe that I walked across the room without my crutches so she demanded I demonstrate it for her. When I promptly repeated my feat, she took the crutches from me permanently. I walk with my prosthesis without a cane or crutches to this day.

Chapter 2

Vicarious Victory

Despite my handicap, sports were a regular part of my life from a very young age, largely because my father loved and coached basketball and my brother played a number of sports throughout his youth. Most of my athletic activity was relegated to driveway basketball with the neighborhood kids, watching games on TV or cheering on my younger brother, Paul, from the bleachers. However, thanks to the courage and encouragement of my father, I did experience a season of organized basketball.

My father, Wilfred Vince, was a very good basketball player in the mid-50s at a small Mississippi high school. He was 6'3" with a long and lanky build. He was probably talented enough to play in college but chose to start a family early in life, marrying my mother at the age of 20. I was born in 1959 – the first of three children.

Two years later my brother Paul was born, and a year after that my sister Debbie arrived. My father's connection to the game of basketball would have to be from the bench rather than on the court.

It was 1969 in West Monroe, Louisiana, a small town about a hundred miles east of Shreveport. My father was coaching my brother's youth basketball team – no minor feat as he was a long-haul truck driver who would be gone for weeks at a time. He would often return from a long trip after we were fast asleep, then sleep during the day and depart for his next trip at night while we were again in bed. Still, during the basketball season he somehow found the time to coach.

I was ten years old that 1969 season and decided I wanted to play basketball with my brother. Although I had given up crutches a few years earlier, I was still not able to run or jump – basic requirements for any basketball player. My old-style prosthetic legs did not bend at the knee, which severely limited my agility and speed. However, my parents never put limits on what I could and couldn't do, never let me use the word "can't" and always told me, "You never know until you try." So rather than dismissing my admittedly odd request to play ball, my father asked the league to let me join my brother's eight-year-old team. The league officials agreed and my short-lived career on the hardwood began.

Despite my handicap, I did more than simply sit the bench. A few games into the season, my father had devised a winning formula that included me on the floor. Rather than hobbling up and down the court with every possession, I was positioned under our basket, camping out there alone on offense and leaving our team short-handed. Since our guards, including Paul, were so good, they were still able to regularly steal the ball and lob it down the court to me for an easy layup. That unconventional play became an important part of our offense.

During one particular game, our defense swiped the ball on four consecutive possessions, passed the ball to me, and I turned it into two points each time. The opposing team's coach, clearly befuddled, called time-out and conferred with his players. His solution was to stick a defender next to me at all times, turning the game into a four-on-four match up on the other end of the floor. The coach's strategy neutralized me as an offensive threat (I didn't score another point) but took away their offensive advantage. The damage was done. We won the game.

My experience on the basketball team was merely one of numerous instances of my parents not setting artificial limits for me, enabling me to build some self-esteem and allowing me to live as normal a childhood as possible. That attitude of support gave me a confidence that I could achieve whatever I set my mind to. It's a confidence that I carried into adulthood and into my baseball coaching career. After all, it takes a healthy amount of self-esteem for a double amputee to choose coaching as a professional career. That self-confidence and toughness was developed early and gradually. I am forever grateful that my parents always believed in my potential, which allowed me to do the same.

There were two other factors that played a very important role in how I handled what I was dealt in life: my acceptance of Jesus Christ as a young boy and the fact that I was born without legs rather than losing them later in life. If I had been born with legs and lost them later in life, I may have never overcome the emotional bitterness that comes with such a traumatic loss. I've seen it happen many times. On more than one occasion I've met people who lost legs in skiing accidents or car wrecks and who simply refused to get prosthetics because of some lingering anger over their ordeal.

Sometimes a mutual friend would ask me to talk to those accident victims about how I have dealt with my disability. Occasionally they would visit one of my baseball team's practices, and they see me standing up on the field with my players, hitting ground balls to my infielders. That served as a clear illustration that they didn't have to be confined to their wheelchair or their scooter. They could live an active and productive life. It's all a matter of perspective. They were choosing to impose artificial limits on themselves.

Still, I understand that my own situation differs considerably. I'm a double amputee who was born that way. I adapted because it's all I've ever known. And I always thought that God could use my situation for some good. There is a scripture, Romans 8:28, in which I have found strength and guidance from an early age. It reads, "We know that in all things God works for the good of those who love him, who have been called according to his purpose." I have tried to do my part to the best of my ability, and God has certainly done His.

***

Despite my successful turn on the elementary basketball circuit, my organized sports career didn't last long. As I grew older, I realized I wouldn't be able to play on the school teams because the competition grew more serious. I still loved athletics, so I looked for ways to remain involved and around sports. I learned how to keep the score books, announced the games on the public address system and learned how to run the scoreboards. Later, while in high school and college, I worked as the student manager and earned two high school letters and two college letters as team manager.

Because I could not physically play the game, I lived vicariously through my brother's athletic successes. Paul continued to play in the baseball and basketball leagues in West Monroe into the 70s, and I took it upon myself to push him to be better. We would play pick-up basketball games until dark every day in our driveway. When baseball season rolled around, I would pitch batting practice to him, hit him ground balls and catch for him while he practiced pitching. By the time Paul was 12, he had grown into an all-star basketball and baseball player. I followed every game as though I were playing myself. When he succeeded, I felt I succeeded.

The pinnacle of Paul's baseball career probably came in his junior year of high school. In the middle of the 1978 school year, our family moved from West Monroe to Lake Charles in the southwest corner of Louisiana. Paul transferred from West Monroe High School to LaGrange High School in Lake Charles. The LaGrange baseball team was enjoying some success that season. Because Paul was new to the team, he began the year out of the starting line-up, getting only spotty playing time. Near mid-season, however, in a non-district game my brother started at second base and went 2 for 3 while making every defensive play that came his way. The coach gave him another opportunity; Paul continued to perform well and eventually became the full-time starter at second base.

LaGrange made it to the state playoffs and played their way to the state semi-finals, where ironically they met West Monroe, the school that Paul had attended at the beginning of that same school year. West Monroe defeated LaGrange that day, ending my brother's season. However, that was the best baseball team still to date that LaGrange has ever had, and my brother had the unique opportunity to be a part of that. I felt like I was an integral part of his success on the field because of all the hours over the years I had put in trying to help him improve his skills. I gained a tremendous amount of satisfaction and pride in his accomplishments.

All those years following his career, I was doing more than cheering. I was constantly around the practices and games of the teams he was playing for and paying attention to the details of techniques the coaches were teaching. I became a student of the game, soaking up all the knowledge I could on how to teach the finer points of baseball. Even after Paul's playing days were over, I continued learning by attending coaching clinics, working college baseball camps and working as the baseball student manager. All these experiences together are what enabled me to become a meticulous teacher of the game as well as a successful game-day strategist.

I owe so much of my early career success to the experience I gained coaching and working with my brother, and I am eternally thankful that he was receptive to my coaching and pushing him to be the best player he could be.

CHAPTER 3

COMMITTING TO COACHING

I graduated from West Monroe High School in 1977 with baseball both in my blood and on my mind. I had closely followed my brother's many successes on the field and had come to appreciate the game and all its nuances. By my graduation, the sport had become a passion of mine. Still, as I started my freshman year of college at Northeast Louisiana University (a four-year college in Monroe now called University of Louisiana at Monroe), I assumed I should take a more practical route and enter a profession that would involve a desk job. The idea of pursing a coaching career had yet to even cross my mind.

This was the 1970s in Louisiana, and the oil industry and chemical industries were enjoying an unprecedented period of growth. Many of my fellow classmates were taking high-paying jobs on oil rigs, in refineries or on the docks. Realizing I would never be able to physically perform these tasks due to my handicapping condition, I rationalized that I needed to find a career field that would provide lucrative pay and a nice desk job. I had taken a bookkeeping class my junior year of high school, so I decided I would major in accounting, which offered good pay and an easy working environment behind a desk.

My practical plan hit a road block early on when I realized accounting was clearly not for me. I struggled in Accounting 101 and Economics 101, barely pulling a C in the latter course. Such difficulty in an intro class concerned me because I had been an A and B student since the sixth grade. I decided to give accounting one more semester, even though by this time it was clear I did not enjoy the subject in the least. By the middle of my second semester, with my grades again faltering, I came to the realization that an accounting major was simply not the path I should take in my life. I withdrew from the classes and soon found myself at a major crossroads without any direction or career path.

I sought counsel from The Reverend Lynn Baggett, a youth pastor at First Baptist Church West Monroe. He was a man I respected. We met at the local Pizza Hut. When I explained to him my dilemma, he looked me straight in the eye and asked me what it was I really wanted to do with my life. I thought about it for a moment and replied that I wanted to coach baseball. It was the first time I had ever told anyone about my desire to coach. At that point, it would have been understandable had my pastor seen me only as a double amputee and kindly steered me toward a more practical profession that could accommodate someone with my physical handicaps. But he did not hesitate; instead he responded immediately that I should major in physical education.

"I can't do that. I'm handicapped," I protested. "Besides, I didn't even take PE in high school."

Reverend Baggett explained that the majority of the course work for a physical education major would be in the classroom, and that I would probably have only four classes that actually involved physical activity. Plus, the instructors would perhaps accommodate my situation. I had kicked the idea around in my head, but I had never considered coaching as a serious career possibility. Yet, this youth pastor was encouraging me to pursue my dream and had confidence that I could make it work. That little nudge in the right direction took me a long way.

In the fall of 1978, I headed further south for a fresh start at McNeese State University in Lake Charles, Louisiana, and changed my academic major to Health and PE. The majority of the course work was indeed classroom based and considerably more interesting to me than the accounting, economics and marketing I had slogged through my previous year. I had to take only four activity classes and, just as my youth pastor had predicted, the instructors made modifications for me – with one memorable exception: my badminton/tennis class.

In my previous activity classes, if I couldn't physically perform the tasks involved in the sport, I was graded on learning the rules and officiating the sport. The tennis instructor, however, would make no such concessions, even though I could not physically run up and down the court or move laterally to hit the tennis ball. The instructor gave me the same skill tests and same grading scale as the other students. I received a C in the class, which at the time seriously upset me. In retrospect, however, I realize it was a sign of respect on the instructor's part towards me. She was simply treating me as a normal student, just like the others in the class. I, like most handicapped people, want respect, not pity. And that's what I got.

In addition to my regular studies, I was the athletic team manager for the McNeese baseball team for two years, for which I earned two athletic letterman awards. I was responsible for packing and unpacking baseball equipment every day for practice and games. During this time I learned a great deal about practice organization, especially for a larger squad of 25 to 30 players. Later when I became a coach with my own team, I would practice my junior varsity and varsity groups together because I was comfortable with my practice organization skills I had learned at McNeese. I also gained a considerable amount of knowledge of game management and strategy.

While I served as team manager, I would often ask Head Coach Johnny Suydam questions about the reasoning behind the decisions he made. I wasn't confrontational and was certainly not second guessing his decisions. He understood that I simply wanted to understand more about the coach's role in the game.

I learned that often times coaches rely on a gut feeling when making in-game decisions, while other times they rely on more concrete information such as scouting reports, statistics and the accepted by-the-book strategies that are generally accepted as correct in the coaching ranks. I wanted to be a sponge and soak up as much detail about in-game strategy and game management as I could because I had never played or coached the game before. Ultimately, the opportunity to be the team manager of a college team and to interact on a personal level with the coaching staff greatly enhanced my coaching career success. I consider it my "playing experience" even though I never stepped into a batter's box or onto a pitcher's mound.

Like my life overall, my college experience was about more than sports alone. I also had the opportunity to explore and develop my lifelong love of music. From my early childhood days I have always enjoyed singing, listening to music on the radio and attending concerts. I sang in the choir and men's ensemble in high school and continued my musical involvement in college, where I was awarded a vocal music major scholarship even though I was a PE major. For four years of college, I performed in the university choir and participated in two operas. I also participated in the McNeese talent show, where I sang a love song duet with classmate Allison Peltz and snagged the first place prize of $100.

My love of music has stayed with me long after my college years. I served as high school choir director at Port Sulphur for two years. We performed at the 1984 World's Fair in New Orleans, on local radio and at the mall in Gretna, Louisiana, during the Christmas holidays. I've also had the pleasure of serving as music director for three different churches over the years, and I sang at my own wedding. I still sing for special events and in churches. What I enjoy most about singing and performing is that, no matter what current mood you're in, you can always find a song with a message that fits the mood or another that can change the mood entirely. I take pride that through my singing I have transcended the stereotypical mold of a single-minded jock who becomes a coach.

I went on to graduate from McNeese State in 1981 with a bachelor's degree in Health and PE with a minor in English. I finished with a GPA of 3.36, despite my C in badminton.

Armed with my degree, some more coaching knowledge and a newfound confidence (in myself and my skills as a coach), I was now ready to pursue my dream of coaching high school baseball. However, there was still a lingering air of uncertainty hovering over me. I couldn't help but wonder if a school would take a chance on a double-amputee coach without any name recognition from a high-profile playing career – or any playing career for that matter.

Thankfully, the answer would be yes.

CHAPTER 4

DARING DECISIONS

I was a 21-year-old head baseball coach at Catholic-Pointe Coupee High School in New Roads, Louisiana, about thirty miles northwest of Baton Rouge, when an angry father came to see me. My new team had stumbled off to an 0-4 start, and the man's son, senior second baseman Keith Boyd, was having a rough stretch of his own. Despite the occasional spectacular play, he was committing far too many errors on routine plays. Feeling a need for more defensive consistency, I made a change, inserting a freshman (future college player Dennis Barker) into the starting line-up at second base and moved the senior to designated hitter. His father was not pleased.

The father had not attended any of the first four games, which meant he hadn't seen his son's defensive issues firsthand. But he was in my office immediately threatening to pull Keith off the team when he learned a freshman was starting in the infield over his son. I tried to convince the father that his son was still in the starting line-up as the DH, that our team would be pretty good (despite the fact the team was 0-4 at the moment), and that I didn't want his son to miss out on our team's success. I asked the father to let his son decide for himself and thankfully Keith decided not to quit. In fact, he would play an important role before season's end. And it would be quite a season.

Despite such a bumpy start to my career, I still felt fortunate to be a head coach only a few months removed from my college graduation. Once college wrapped up, I had the opportunity to choose between two teaching and coaching offers. The first was from Marvin Holland, the athletic director and head coach at Zachary High School, just north of Baton Rouge. There I would be an assistant for the football and baseball teams. The other offer was from Jim Hightower, the athletic director and head football coach at Catholic-Pointe Coupee, where I would be an assistant football coach and head baseball coach. Although Zachary High School was a public institution and offered a higher salary, I felt the opportunity to be a head coach right out of college, especially as a double amputee, was simply too good to pass up.

I was very apprehensive, to say the least, because I had never coached football before or even been around football teams. My only exposure to the sport was as a spectator, either attending games or watching it on television. I knew the learning curve for me would be very steep. Fortunately, the other coaches on the staff were very strong football coaches and the team was full of talented players. In fact, coaching football helped me transition into my first year as head baseball coach because many of my baseball players also played on the football team. By the time baseball season rolled around, I was familiar with many of the players, and they were familiar with me.

Heading into that first baseball season, there was cause for both optimism and apprehension on my part. The year prior to my arrival, the team had made it to the Class A state semifinals, and many of the players from that team would be returning. However, the school was moving up to the significantly more competitive Class AA, and we opened the season with a tournament against even bigger schools in higher classifications. Given the team's success the previous year, losing our first four games was cause for much concern for everybody around the program. Add in the fact that I was a young coach, so I'm sure there was considerable apprehension about whether or not I could get the job done. Still, I maintained confidence in myself and in my team.

My faith in the team was well placed. Our reconfigured roster started to come together almost immediately and went on an amazing run of 22 straight wins and entered the Class AA playoffs riding high. During our opening round playoff game against Vandebilt Catholic, senior DH Keith Boyd got the game winning double. The freshman who took his place at second, Dennis Barker, helped turn a 6-4-3 double play with the tying run at third base in the bottom of the seventh inning for the final outs.

We cruised to the semifinal game, which turned into a major battle. During that game, we jumped out to a quick 6-0 lead in the early innings before our starting pitcher and staff ace, lefty Paul Chustz, gave up two 3-run homers in the third inning, allowing the other team to tie the game. I inserted our Number 2 pitcher into the game, John Rodney, and he shut down our opponent for six innings until we secured the game in the 9th.

Next up was John Curtis, a New Orleans-area school with a long athletic tradition. The championship game was the next day and our pitching rotation was well positioned to give us a competitive advantage. However, I made a rookie mental mistake that I believe squandered that edge. I haphazardly figured that, since I pitched my top two pitchers the day before, I couldn't throw them the next day. But what I should have remembered was that my ace lasted only three innings the game before, and he was still able to pitch in the championship game. For some reason, that thought never entered my mind. Instead, I started our Number 3 pitcher, and we promptly found ourselves down 5-2 by the fifth inning. I pulled the starter and replaced him with John Rodney. John pitched a shutout the rest of the way.

With our pitching under control, our bats eventually came to life. We found ourselves down to our last at bat and behind by three runs, and we loaded the bases for our best hitter Scott Devillier. Scott slammed a pitch deep in the right centerfield gap that appeared as if it will be a game winning grand slam. Steve Stropolo, John Curtis's center fielder who had tremendous speed, was cheating toward left center gap in anticipation of Scott pulling the ball that way. The ball sailed toward the fence. I held my breath.

"Surely he can't cover that much ground," I thought to myself.

I was wrong. Not only did Stropolo make it to the fence, but he reached over the fence and made a leaping grab to rob Scott of a grand slam and snatch the state championship from our grasp. That day we were mere inches away from the state championship. It just wasn't to be for us that day.

C.H.S.P.C. Green Hornet Baseball Team

**CLASS 2-A CATHOLIC POINT COUPEE HIGH SCHOOL
1982 AA STATE RUNNER-UP—FIRST TEAM I EVER COACHED
PHOTO: THANKS TO THE *POINTE COUPEE BANNER***

Many coaches have long coaching careers and never have the opportunity to play for a state championship and yet there I was, a fresh-faced double amputee doing it my very first year coaching. The next year, after losing quite a few players, we would finish 18-9, losing to Opelousas Catholic 1-0 in the quarterfinals. My combined won-loss record for those first two years was 40-13 – not too bad of a career start for someone who never physically played the game.

Still, I can say with certainty that baseball was not the best thing that happened to me in New Roads during those two years.

When I first took the job in New Roads, I still had a girlfriend back in Lake Charles who was attending McNeese. In New Roads, being on my own for the first time, I usually did my grocery shopping at the local Winn Dixie. Every time I shopped at the store I always ended up in this one particular young woman's cashier's line. In passing conversation she knew I was a coach and always knew how my team had fared that week. I never paid much attention to it or thought much about it because I was in a relationship. Plus, working as a coach in a small town is like being a fish in a bowl: everybody

 knows who you are and how you are doing.

After my first year on the job, the long distance relationship wasn't panning out and I broke up with my girlfriend. Unfortunately for me, New Roads, with a population of less than 5,000, wasn't exactly brimming with single young women. A coaching buddy of mine suggested that I go down to the softball park on Tuesday nights for the ladies softball league. I took his advice. To my surprise, there were quite a few kids I taught and coached from school hanging out at the park, and I spent most of the night talking with them rather than watching the ladies on the field.

After chatting for a while, I noticed a young lady standing off to the side patiently waiting to speak to me. She stood there ten minutes or so waiting for my conversations with the students to end. When they finally did, she approached me and smiled.

"Do you know who I am?" she asked.

"I don't know your name," I replied, smiling back. "But I know you're a cashier at Winn Dixie. I always end up in your line."

Her name was Susan LeCoq. As we talked that night, we discovered we had a lot in common. Susan had been a cheerleader, played softball and ran track in high school. She was at the park that night playing recreational softball. Naturally, someone who enjoyed and understood sports would easily attract my attention. That very night I asked her if she would attend an athletic banquet for my team later that week. She accepted immediately. Later, she attended my summer team's baseball games and would often keep the score book for the games. We continued to date the remainder of the year and our relationship quickly blossomed.

At the end of my second year coaching, I decided to leave New Roads to accept a higher-paying position at

Port Sulphur High in the southeast corner of the state. I didn't want to leave Susan behind because long distance relationships hadn't worked for me. I knew she was the right one for me so I proposed to her in the summer of 1983. We were married December 17, 1983.

It takes a special woman to be a coach's wife. Coaches' wives have to put up with the time demands that being a successful coach requires, the travel, the coaching clinics and much more. Couple that with the fact that I'm a double amputee, she was still willing to marry me. She believed in me and she wholeheartedly supported my coaching career. In retrospect, I believe it wasn't just coincidence that I always went through her checkout line at Winn Dixie, but rather part of God's plan for my life. I've truly been blessed to have Susan as my wife.

26TH WEDDING ANNIVERSARY
SUNSET DINNER CRUISE, 2010
CLEARWATER

CHAPTER 5

COLLEGE COACHING CHALLENGES

After two successful years at Catholic Pointe Coupee in New Roads, I moved on to Port Sulphur High School among the bayous of far southeast Louisiana. We won our district championship two years in a row, and I was named West Bank Coach of the Year by the *Times-Picayune* newspaper.

Over those first four years, I had proven to myself and others that I could coach at a high level despite never having played the game myself. With that new experience and confidence in hand, I set my sights on a more ambitious goal: coaching college baseball. From the moment I first stepped into a dugout as a coach, my ultimate career goal was to lead a baseball team in the college ranks, and it was a goal I was willing to take chances to achieve. That is how in 1983 I came to accept a position of graduate assistant at Henderson State University in Arkadelphia, Arkansas, a small town about an hour southwest of Little Rock.

To take the position, I gave up a comfortable annual salary for a $3,600 yearly stipend and free tuition. It was certainly a sacrifice, but it brought me one step closer to my dream. Susan worked as a cashier at the local Piggly Wiggly grocery store to help ends meet as I pursued my goal and worked toward my master's degree, which I finished in a year.

At HSU I taught golf classes to undergraduates and served as recruiting coordinator for the baseball team during the day. In the afternoons I was assistant baseball coach, and at night I would take my own master's classes. And for one brief moment, I served as head coach – an incident that is forever etched in my mind.

During the regular season, our team finished in second place and entered the conference tournament as the Number 2 seed, where we faced our opening round opponent. Early in the game, with our team up by several runs, Head Coach Dr. Clyde Berry did as baseball coaches will occasionally do: he passionately argued a call and promptly got himself ejected from the game. That meant I, as the only assistant coach, had to take over the team. I took my place in the third base coaching box for the remainder of the inning and returned to the dugout. Little did I know those few minutes would spark a major controversy – and that the fight would be over something as seemingly trivial as the clothes I was wearing that would set off the situation.

When I started my coaching career, the Louisiana High School Athletic Association rules did not require baseball coaches to be in uniform. Most baseball coaches would wear a collared shirt with a school logo with a pair of coaching shorts. I usually wore the same but with a pair of dress slacks. I never gave it much thought other than the fact it would be a major inconvenience for me to get dressed and undressed in baseball uniform pants before and after games. However, I would definitely think about it that day in Arkansas.

Once the inning ended, the opposing head coach complained to the umpire that coaches were to be in full uniform and because I wasn't, he argued that we should immediately forfeit the game. I guess he figured since his team was losing at the time, this was his only chance at victory. When I realized what was happening, I pleaded my case with the umpires, informing them that I was a double amputee who wears two artificial legs and that the wearing of baseball uniform pants created an undue hardship for me. I pleaded that what I was wearing was not going to be a determining factor in who would win and that we should let the players, not my blue jeans, determine the outcome of the game. Fortunately, reason prevailed and the umpires decided the game would continue to completion. Still, the opposing coach lodged an official protest, which was rendered moot once the opposing team rallied to defeat us and subsequently ended our season.

It was a frustrating but instructive experience for me. I considered this complaint and the coach's protest to be a personal slap in the face, an act of desperation and an example of a "win at all cost mentality." I vowed to never take such a classless approach as a coach. From that moment on in my coaching career, I wore a full baseball uniform, whether the rules required it or not. I decided I would not allow something as silly as the type of pants I was wearing to cost my team a victory. My teams work too hard to have a win stripped from them on a technicality, regardless of the inconvenience it causes me.

***

Once I completed my master's degree in August of 1986, I was offered and accepted the position of Head Baseball Coach at Campbellsville University in Campbellsville, Kentucky. At the age of 26, and only five years into my coaching career, I had achieved my dream of becoming a head college baseball coach. We went on to win the Kentucky Intercollegiate Athletic Conference championship in dramatic fashion, and I was named KIAC coach of the year. Those successes ultimately made for a memorable year, but our team experienced and overcame a tragedy along the way that has proven just as memorable as the championships and accolades.

On a Saturday in April, we had a conference double-header in Pikeville, about four hours east of Campbells-ville. Our starting left fielder was an 18-year-old fresh-man, Andy Patterson. That day Andy was mowing his church's lawn prior to catching the team bus for our trip. Andy didn't quite finish the job and asked his father to complete what little he had left because he had to leave for the game.

We traveled the four hours, won both games of the doubleheader and made the four-hour trek home the same day, arriving back in Campbellsville around midnight. As our bus pulled into the campus parking lot, I noticed something highly unusual. There was a crowd of around a hundred people waiting to greet our return. We hadn't clinched a playoff or won a championship yet, and a crowd had never greeted our bus before, certainly not at midnight.

The second I stepped off the bus, it became clear. Andy Patterson's father had finished mowing the church lawn after Andy left, returned home, drank a glass of ice tea, laid down for a nap and suffered a massive heart attack in his sleep, passing away.

This is one of the toughest things I would experience in my entire coaching career. Here I was, only 26 years old and having to inform a young player of mine that he had lost his father. As you might expect, Andy took the news very hard and blamed himself for his father's death. He felt at the time that had he finished mowing the church lawn himself, this would have never happened. As a team and his second family, we tried to be there for him, offering words of comfort, encouragement, and bringing the entire team to the funeral. In times like these, finding the right words to say are often hard to come by. We were determined, however, to show Andy we cared for him and his family, and we would be available to him for whatever he would need. Although something this tragic and sudden is tough to handle, I feel our team rallying to support Andy and his family strengthened our team bond, enabling us to draw closer to one another as a baseball family.

I learned an important life lesson through this experience. The most important things in coaching are the relationships and bonds formed among players and coaches. Sure, wins and losses and X's and O's are important, but they are secondary to a caring, trusting player/coach relationship. It became very important to me that my players know that I cared for them and would be there for them as a human being and not just for what they could accomplish on a baseball diamond.

Unfortunately, this would not be the last time one of my players would experience a sudden loss of a family member. Four years later, while coaching at Ellender High School in Houma, Louisiana, tragedy would strike again. We were at practice going through our daily practice drills and routines when I noticed a lady walking right into the middle of the field. I didn't recognize this person and remember saying to myself, "who is this person and what is she doing interrupting my practice!"

I would be ashamed and embarrassed of these thoughts once she identified herself and the reason for her visit. The lady was the mother of Spencer Duplantis, a reserve outfielder for our team. She was there to pick up Spencer because, just moments earlier, Spencer's 20-year-old brother was killed in a car wreck. My heart sank. Only a few minutes prior to Spencer's mom arriving to our practice, my entire team heard the noise of screeching tires and then the loud bang of a collision. Although we could not see the accident, it certainly was loud enough that our team had a pause in our practice, then continued on with our business. To later learn that the victim in that accident was a teammate's brother was just gut wrenching

Although I didn't know and had never met Spencer's brother, I felt compelled to attend the wake and be there for Spencer. A few days after the funeral, Spencer's mother revealed to me how touched and moved and filled with gratitude Spencer was that I attended his brother's wake. For me, it just was the right thing to do. Spencer may not remember how many games we won or lost during those years, but I hope he will always remember his coach cared enough about him to attend his brother's wake.

Another life lesson I learned through this experience is to never take for granted the power of influence a coach can have on his players. I had often preached to players that it is the little things that make a huge difference.

Despite winning the conference championship and KIAC coach of the year honors in Campbellsville, I was let go at the end of the season. It was simply a matter of being at the right place at the wrong time.

Schools are subject to accreditation reviews every ten years. For colleges and universities, one of the rules is that each department within the university must have 10 percent of its faculty members possess a doctoral degree. Prior to my arrival at Campbellsville, Dr. Danny Davis was the only health department faculty member with a doctoral degree. Unfortunately for me, he was the faculty member I replaced when he accepted a position at the University of North Carolina-Pembroke. Because all other faculty members within this department possessed master's degrees, the HPER department faced losing its accredited status – a devastating blow for any institution. To avoid this, the administration had to hire a faculty member with a doctoral degree. Since I was the most recent employee hired within the department, I was the first let go to make room for the new hire.

I started my job search immediately, but soon realized it would be more difficult than I anticipated to land another college position. There was certainly interest from a number of schools. In fact, over a four-month period I was a finalist for five other college jobs.

When athletic directors are trying to decide between two equally qualified candidates, one being handicapped and one not being handicapped, I would think the easier decision and human nature would lean toward the non-handicapped candidate. I am not so naïve to believe that I was the perfect candidate for every position I applied for. I am also sure that, at the time, the athletic directors believed they had chosen the right man for the job. After I finished second five times in a row over a four-month period, however, it did make me wonder if my handicap was a determining factor. And for one job in particular, I firmly believe it was.

One of the first positions I interviewed for after Campbellsville was a university in northeast Indiana. The athletic director and I agreed to begin the interview with a breakfast in a local restaurant and proceed from there to the university. I arrived very early and made sure I was seated well in advance of the athletic director's arrival. As is always the case when I apply for jobs, I did not mention my handicapping condition on my resume, which meant our initial conversation should have focused on baseball and coaching rather than my artificial legs.

I found that my credentials and proven track record of success usually landed me in the top five candidates for most coaching positions for which I applied. I never tried to hide my condition from potential employees. It's just that I always felt that once I can meet a potential employer face to face, I can use my handicap as more of a positive than a negative. I can explain that everything I accomplished and listed in my resume was achieved despite my handicap. Furthermore, I can point out that my handicap was a result of a birth defect and that for my entire life I have been an overachiever who has consistently defied expectations. I let them know they will get a coach who will not be held back by ordinary obstacles or problems, someone who will make the best of the tools available to me and the circumstances with which I am faced.

When the Indiana athletic director arrived at the restaurant, he walked over and warmly introduced himself to me. We shook hands.

"I see you have a handicapped plate on your truck. Can you tell me about that" was the very next thing out of his mouth.

I was floored that this was the first thing he mentioned. I realized he knew I was driving from Kentucky and must have noticed that the other vehicles in the parking lot had Indiana plates. The only Kentucky vehicle in the lot was mine, and yes, it had a handicapped plate.

It caught me off guard that he so abruptly asked the question, in no small part because it was technically illegal. Still, I remained confident I could hold fast to my plan and shed a positive light on my condition. I couldn't have been more wrong. I could tell by the athletic director's facial expressions and body language that I would not be seriously considered for the job. Although we continued with the interview, taking the tour of the university and its athletic facilities, I felt like everything I said after his initial question fell on deaf ears. I didn't get the job.

Because of my faith, I just chalked this setback to it simply not being God's will for my life, and I opted to not file an EEO complaint of discrimination. I'm certain in this case, however, my handicap was a determining factor in me not landing the position.

Situations like this make me thankful for the many special people who throughout my career were willing to take a risk and hire a double-amputee baseball coach. They were able to look past my handicap and see me as a complete person and coach. For that, I will always be grateful.

CHAPTER 6

INTERNATIONAL BASEBALL EXPERIENCES

As a young child I remember seeing TV newscasts of our military personnel returning home from war. One of the first things the soldiers did after descending the stairs from the airplane was kiss the U.S. soil. Being young, immature, and naive at the time, I often laughed and ridiculed those actions.

It wasn't until I first traveled overseas into foreign countries that I gained a new perspective, new insight, and greater appreciation for America, the greatest country in the world. After seeing foreign countries up close and personal, it's no wonder people risk their lives and their life's savings to reach the United States of America.

Here are a few stories from my first experiences overseas in 1988 that helped hammer into my heart a greater appreciation for my country.

My first international baseball trip was with a group called Athletes in Action, which is a Christian organization that uses sports as a tool to spread the gospel of Christ. I would serve as the head baseball coach of the Athletes in Action Europe 1988 baseball team that would be comprised of college players from all over the United States. On this trip we would spend one week each in the countries of Spain, Czechoslovakia, Holland, and Sweden. The mission of this trip was to provide baseball clinics, play games against local club teams, pass out gospel tracts, and share personal testimonies at all of our events to both the audience and the players.

Our first stop was Bilboa, Spain. We were treated like royalty there. I believe we were the first ever American sports team to travel to that region of Spain. We were mobbed by the crowds every time we loaded or unloaded our bus, our games were broadcast on local TV stations and radio stations. This made us all feel like major leaguers.

While in Spain, we were always reminded to not drink the water because it was not sanitary like it is for drinking water in the United States. The problem for me was I never drink alcohol of any kind. Yet wine, which I refused, was being served at every meal. The other option was to drink sodas at $3 a can. In 1988 coke was 50 cents back home, and I didn't want to spend that kind of money on coke, so I drank the water. This will bite me later.

After spending four days in Bilboa, we traveled to Barcelona, Spain. Barcelona was the host for the 1992 Olympics, and we were there in 1988 witnessing all the construction and preparations taking place. We received a radically different reception in Barcelona. It was as if no one knew we were there. Very sparse crowds attended our games or events, which was totally opposite the heroes' welcome we received in Bilboa.

While in Barcelona, our team went to the bullfights. What a spectacle! While we were there, one of the fighters made an error and was gored in the leg. These gladiators of Spain received the accolades that so many of our American sport professionals receive.

By now, having been drinking the water for almost a full week, I began having diarrhea. We were downtown near the beautiful fountains, and I needed to find a rest room. Through an interpreter I learned a rest room was two blocks away, so I made my way to its location. To my surprise when I arrived, there was a young lady sitting with a money bowl between the two rest rooms. Apparently, you have to pay to use the public rest rooms in Spain. I had left my money with my wife, and I knew I'd never make it in time to return to my wife and back to rest room. I went into the bathroom and just hoped that maybe she would be on break when I came out. I was in the rest room quite some time and, when I did leave, the money collector was gone.

When we left Spain, our next stop was going to be Prague, Czechoslovakia. We had to change planes in the Frankfurt, Germany airport. This is an airport that has been attacked by terrorists multiple times. It was eye opening to see the security guards walking around with uzi machine guns and ammunition belts strapped to their shoulders. In addition to that disconcerting sight, our departure gate for our plane was right next to the departure gate for a plane leaving for Iran. You will recall 1988 was not that far removed from the Iranian Crisis where 44 U.S. hostages were held. Yet, here we are, a large group of Americans right next to a large group of Iranians waiting for planes in the same general area. To say tensions were high on my part is an understatement.

Czechoslovakia was still a communist country in 1988. Our plane to Prague was an old World War II war plane now in service as airline carrier Czech Air. It was not a very smooth or comfortable ride. We were concerned about whether our luggage would be checked. In our possession were gospel tracts, Bibles written in the Czech language and a Jesus film in their language, all of which were illegal for us to bring in. Fortunately not one of our bags was inspected. Ironically, though, a team from Italy was driving in and were stopped for 2 - 1/2 hours and every car and bag was checked.

When we left Czechoslovakia, our bags were searched but by then we had distributed the material and were returning with only souvenirs. The most popular souvenirs were the wooden Russian dolls and crystal glassware.

While in the early days of being in Czechoslovakia, I was still experiencing diarrhea from Spain water. I found myself at a city bus station needing the rest room.

Inside the rest room all the stalls were locked. Another gentlemen who didn't speak English recognized my dilemma, and he pointed to some wooden, locked windows. He gave me a hand signal indicating that I should knock. When I knocked on the window, a middle-aged woman opened the window, handed me three sheets of wax paper, then came around into the men's rest room and unlocked the stall. You guessed it. The three pieces of wax paper was to be my toilet paper.

An interesting and moving event happened daily at the ball games. Very few people there spoke English but the ball games had a DJ playing American music. Through an interpreter I asked if the crowd understands the words to the songs they were playing. He said no, they just liked the rhythms and the beat. Well as luck would have it, my team is getting ready to play against a team from Russia. While we were taking our pre-game infield practice, the DJ played Bruce Springsteen's "Born in the USA." Chill bumps raced up and down my spine. I was so filled with national pride. A USA vs. Russia ball game being played in a communist country with "Born in the USA" blaring from the sound system. It was a memory of a lifetime for me.

Our next stop would be Amsterdam, Holland. Amsterdam claims to have the lowest crime rate in the world. Travel there and you understand why. Most everything is not illegal. Prostitution is a government-regulated business, drug sales and drug possession are legal and done openly on the streets and in pharmacies all over town. As a career high school English teacher, I taught the novel, *The Diary of Anne Frank* every year. A thrilling moment for me during my travels to Holland was my opportunity to walk in the very building and see first hand the setting for that novel.

Our baseball team was winning our games by fairly large margins so our host Czech team challenged us to a game in their sport of soccer. As fate would have it, my starting second baseman attempts to head a ball, misses it and butts heads with a Czech player. Next thing I know, two men are getting into a heated argument with my player standing in the middle of them. Once I got an interpreter over there, he explained to me what the argument was about. My player was going to need stitches to repair the gash above his eye. One gentleman wanted to stitch him right there on the spot, and the other man was arguing that our player needed to go to the hospital to get stitches.

Well that was a no-brainer decision that I made for them: he's going to the hospital. Remember, this is 1988 Communist Czechoslovakia. The hospital was crude and not up to American standards. Nevertheless, my player took six stitches above his eye, and we no longer engaged in any more soccer games on the trip.

The final stop was Stockholm, Sweden. Several interesting things occurred while we were there. While in Czechoslovakia, we were constantly hearing Bruce Springsteen music played over the sound system. While in Stockholm, Bruce Springsteen appeared in concert there. Several of our players hung out in the parking lot of the stadium he was playing in and recorded his concert.

I stayed with a host family that was deaf. Sweden is one of the few countries that has socialized medicine. This family's house was set up so that if the doorbell rang, a certain color light would blink on/off. If the phone was ringing, a different color would flash. They would pick up the phone and could read teletype what the person on the other end was saying. We are starting to see some of that technology now in America, but in 1988 Sweden already provided that service in full force. Not only was the family's house rigged like this free of charge, but their son had torn his knee up playing softball and had three knee surgeries at no cost. I say at no cost, but the Swedes pay an income tax of 80 percent to have free socialized medicine. Certainly a different perspective.

Another more frightening event occurred while in Sweden. One day my host family was driving me around sightseeing, and we drove by the American Embassy. To our dismay, we noticed a rather large protest rally occurring. People were burning American flags and our president in effigy. Because the newspapers and TV broadcasts were in a language I couldn't understand, I had no clue as to what triggered this anger. Later, I had an interpreter explain to me that a U.S. military plane had shot down an Iranian commercial airliner plane by mistake, triggering the outrage. We would be flying back home in a few more days, and I knew Iran would probably retaliate. We would be traveling right back through that Frankfurt, Germany airport. I was never more relieved and thankful in my life to learn that the airline we would be flying would be foreign carrier Lufthuansa and not an American-based airline.

This first experience in international travel for me opened my eyes to other cultures and some of the hardships people from other countries face. I learned that we Americans take so many things for granted in this country. Americans like their drinks cold, Europeans drink everything hot. Ice costs extra. We don't hesitate to drink water from faucets, water hoses, and fountains, but some countries' drinking water is not fit to drink. We don't pay any attention to toilet paper; we just buy it and use it, yet I was given wax paper for toilet paper in Prague. Items like medical care and soft drink sodas are luxuries in these other countries many can't afford.

After being gone for six weeks out of the U.S., I returned home with a greater appreciation for America. I now understand why those soldiers kissed the ground of U.S. soil upon their return. For everyone who gripes and complains about our country, and our country certainly does have its problems, I challenge you to spend one week in a foreign country. I guarantee you will gain a different perspective and acquire a greater appreciation for America and its blessings.

Once I got a taste of other cultures on that first trip, I yearned for more opportunities that would further educate me and enhance my abilities to relate to and with people of all diversities.

Baseball afforded me opportunities to later coach in Australia, Puerto Rico four times, Italy, Curacao, and Hawaii.

USA ATHLETES INTERNATIONAL
IN CURACAO 2009

MORE INTERNATIONAL BASEBALL EXPERIENCES

Ever since the Crocodile Dundee movies came out, I was infatuated with traveling to Australia. In 2002 that dream became a reality when I was afforded the opportunity to coach baseball there for almost two weeks with Coast to Coast Baseball.

Once again, I traveled with a group of high school-aged players from all over the United States to the beach resort town of Glenelg. Glenelg is about thirty miles south of the city of Adelaide in South Australia.

Summertime in America is winter time in Australia, and we were there in July. Temperatures most days would be in the 60s and overcast with a drizzly rain. One of the toughest things to adjust to was the grueling 26-hour trip and the 14-hour time zone adjustment. To keep from getting our nights and days mixed up, we did not allow our team members to go to bed that first day until 9 p.m. Needless to say, we didn't have any issues with curfew violators after such a grueling trip.

There is an interest in baseball in Australia, although the most popular sports are rugby, soccer and basketball. There was a South Australia Sports Institute training facility that is used to develop baseball skills in players of all ages. The fields where our games were being played were very close to an airport. There were large commercial planes constantly flying at very low altitudes. It reminded me of Shea Stadium, home stadium of the Mets in New York. There have been a couple of players from Australia reach the big leagues in recent years.

We enjoyed a trip to the zoo where we got to see a Tasmanian devil, feed the kangaroos, and hold a koala bear. One had to be very careful around the kangaroos for sometimes, if startled, they would rise on their hind legs and begin to kick at you. Kangaroos are so plentiful in Australia we would often see them along the roadside in the wild. To my surprise, they are also served as a menu item on the local Chinese buffet.

A daily train ran a regular schedule back and forth from the beach resort of Glenelg to the city of Adelaide. Most of us took advantage of this opportunity during our free time to sightsee. The money exchange rate was in our favor in 2002 as we received $2 Australian money for every $1 American money. This afforded us the means to purchase more souvenirs and snacks. My favorite souvenir was a Crocodile Dundee hat with a band of crocodile teeth across the front. If you've seen any of the movies, you know what the hat looks like.

Early in the week, I noticed a restaurant in Glenelg that was named "The B B Que." I didn't give it much thought and didn't surmise that it would be very good. Later in the week, though, I decided to check this place out. It was not a Barb-B-Que place like we think of in the south. It was a steak restaurant. Had I done my research on Australian history, I would have known that Australia is well known for its quality cattle and beef. Like many high-end steak houses in the United States, you can look in the windows and see the sizes and choice cuts you would like to choose from. This place was exactly like that. You select your choice steak and sides, and the cooks would grill it for you. Hence, the name B B Que. The major difference was the price. These selections that would cost $40 to $60 in the United States were only $12 to $20 in Australia. You can imagine that once I discovered this place for what it truly was, the remainder of my free time meals were eaten there.

South Australia is also famous for its wine country and vineyards, as well as a small town famous for its chocolate. We were able to make sight-seeing trips into these areas as well. There are very few countries outside the United States that people can say are truly American friendly. Australians are a very hospitable people. I would welcome the opportunity to return one day to visit Melbourne, Sidney, and the outback.

***

In 2008 I was given the opportunity to experience travel to Italy as coach with USAAI. On this trip we visited some outstanding histori-cal sites. In Rome we saw the Roman Forum, the Pantheon, the Colosseum, Trevi Fountain, St. Peter's Basilica, and the Sistine Chapel. In Florence we saw the Duomo, in Pisa we saw the Lean-ing Tower of Pisa. We also trav-eled to Arrezzo and to the Italian Riviera.

ROMAN COLOSSEUM

Upon our immediate arrival in Rome, we were taken directly to St. Peter's Square and the Vatican City to spend the day sight-seeing. For dinner that first night, we were taken to a local Italian restaurant for a real Italian meal. Our rides to the restaurant were in a Mercedes Benz. What a thrill for most all of us who had never ridden in a Mercedes before.

Much like the South Australia Sports Institute, there is an athletic training facility that is the headquarters for the Italy Olympic Training teams. My team would play against the Junior Olympic baseball team sponsored by major league baseball. What a thrill to be able to compete against that caliber of competition. Our team won one game against them and lost a one-run game against them. The Italy team we competed against left for the Junior Olympic competition in Canada the next week.

We then toured by boat several seaside resorts nestled into the rocks and cliffs along the Italian Riviera. After a brief stay at a beach, we returned for one final night stay in Rome.

Chapter 7

From the Peak to the Valley

After my abrupt departure from Campbellsville and those five near misses with other college jobs, I found myself still unemployed as summer turned to autumn and the school year began. Because I was adamant about staying at the college level, I had not applied for any high school jobs. By October, two months after the start of the school calendar, my prospects of even landing a high school job were bleak, to say the least.

Fortunately, a position eventually opened up at False River Academy back in New Roads, the small town where my coaching career first began. This time around, my duties at False River included assistant football coach, head girls basketball coach, head baseball coach, yearbook sponsor and English teacher. False River was part of the Louisiana Independent School Association rather than the more prestigious Louisiana High School Athletic Association, which sanctioned most of the state's high school sports. The LISA Association member schools were all smaller private schools. It was about as far away from college baseball as I could be.

Initially, I lamented that I had fallen from the high point of being a conference champion head college baseball coach to, in a sense, the lowest point possible. While I was certainly very thankful to even have a job, there was no denying that I was also quite disappointed to drop down so far from the college ranks. Rather than sulk about my circumstances, however, I decided to make the best of the situation I was dealt.

During my time at False River, my coaching success continued. The football team and the baseball team both reached the state semifinals and the girls basketball team also made the playoffs. Two players from my baseball team had highly successful baseball careers after False River. Jerry Dupre went on to play baseball for Mississippi State and Chad Olinde played at Northeast Louisiana University (now called the University of Louisiana at Monroe). Chad, who played one year of pro ball with the Chicago Cubs minor league organizations, is now the head baseball coach at Claiborne Christian Academy in West Monroe, Louisiana. His baseball teams have recently won three consecutive Class C state championships. I'm very proud to have played a small role in their successful careers.

Although it was far away from the bright lights of college baseball, several positive things came out of my time at False River. The head football coach at the school at that time was Chipper Gajan. Chipper and I discovered very quickly that we shared a common passion for not only coaching but also fishing. Although our careers would soon take different paths (Chipper is now an insurance agent for Farm Bureau), we have developed a lifelong friendship that still exists today. On that same coaching staff was a young coach by the name of Dale Luckett. Little did I know that at the time I was coaching with my future brother-in-law. A few years later Dale would marry my wife's youngest sister. Dale is still coaching at South Terrebonne High School in Bourg, Louisiana.

I was intent on working my way back up the coaching ladder, and I left False River in 1989 to accept a position at a 4A LHSAA institution in Houma, Ellender High School. While I didn't have much athletic coaching success during the three years I was there, I did develop some very meaningful personal relationships with players and students.

Ellender is where I began teaching special education classes and earned a teaching certification in that subject area to go along with my certifications already held in English, Health and PE. It helped me develop a very special and rewarding relationship with one of my special education students.

Ryan Burnett was a remarkable quadriplegic cerebral palsy student with a mind as sharp as a razor. He also loved sports, so we immediately hit it off. With permission from Ryan's mom, I made Ryan an honorary baseball team manager and carried him with us to our games. Because his motorized wheelchair would not fit on the school bus, my players would pick up Ryan and carry him on and off the bus, then push him around in a manual wheelchair. This was a great experience for my baseball players. It taught them a great deal about having respect for those less fortunate than themselves and to not take for granted their own physical abilities. Not once did my players gripe or complain about having to push or carry Ryan. They loved being around Ryan as much as Ryan loved being around us.

In the classroom, I was able to get Ryan on a computerized GED program for students with special needs. Within one year, Ryan was able to pass the GED exam and receive his diploma, which was an amazing accomplishment. I am still in touch with Ryan today. He is a season ticket holder for the New Orleans Saints. More importantly, Ryan is a great example of positive human spirit. He loves life, despite his handicapping condition, and I am eternally grateful to have been a small part of his life.

After three years of little success on the field, I left Ellender and moved to Harrison Central High School, a 5A school in the beach town of Gulfport, Mississippi. I led the baseball program at Harrison Central from 1992 to 1996. I have a number of fond memories of coaches I worked with while at Harrison Central. Karl Friedrich and I shared a classroom together. Jimmy Parker worked as one of my assistant baseball coaches and has gone on to win several state championships as head softball coach. Larry Strohm was a coach at the middle school and has become a lifelong friend. Leon Farmer worked as a volunteer assistant for me and would later come with me as an assistant to Port Arthur, Texas. Sadly, a few years ago Leon passed away unexpectedly. He is sorely missed.

Several of my players at Harrison Central received baseball scholarships: Cedric Theodore, Eric Hogue, and Jeremy Delmas. Michael Degruy was selected in the major league baseball draft. These players and coaches all represent happy memories from that time.

Unfortunately, the most lasting memory from that time in Gulfport is a deeply sad one. My father had retired from Lowe's as assistant manager in 1991. In 1992 he had his first heart attack but survived it. During his recovery, he joked that if retirement was going to trigger a heart attack maybe he needed to go back to work. In 1993 he bought a meat market/convenience store and worked there until 1994. In 1994 he went to work for Stine Lumber, a regional hardware chain. After his first heart attack, he started going to the cardiologist for regular checkups. He was given a clean bill of health every time.

On a fall Sunday morning in 1995, I was sitting in the choir loft at church, my usual place every Sunday morning. My wife was working at a construction company in Gulfport at the time and had to work that particular

Sunday. My sister, Debbie, had been trying to reach me most of the morning with no luck. Eventually, she was able to reach my wife at work to inform her that my dad had suffered another heart attack. She left work immediately and headed to the church to deliver the news to me. She came to a side door of the choir loft, got my attention and mouthed the words, "Your daddy has had a heart attack, and we need to leave right now."

Throughout the four-hour drive to the hospital in Lake Charles we were wondering whether he was going to still be alive when we got there. Would we make it in time, but my father was already in a coma. He never regained consciousness, and after a week in the hospital, he passed away.

Because my dad had just received a good report from his cardiologist the week before he died, his heart attack and subsequent death were greatly unexpected, which made the grieving process even more difficult. I don't want to minimize anyone's loss of a loved one, but often if someone has a lengthy illness and is diagnosed as terminal, it offers some time for loved ones to emotionally prepare for the loss. Such was not the case with Dad.

It was a difficult period for my family. Only a few years earlier, my wife's mother was diagnosed with breast cancer at age 44. Doctors gave her six months to live, but she went downhill fast and passed away after only three months. Both my wife and I experiencing a loss of a parent at such young ages was a tremendously trying experience. The love and comfort of our church family and extended baseball family, along with the grace of God, enabled both Susan and me to be strong and to eventually heal from the wounds of such sudden losses.

Still, my father's sudden death is something that continues to affect me in small ways. He was only 55 when he passed away. His father had died at age 50 of a heart attack. I turned 52 in December of 2011. In the back of my mind, I can't help but wonder about my life expectancy – so much so that I scheduled an appointment with a cardiologist in my late forties. I was not physically capable of a treadmill test, but I was given injections that accelerated my heart rate for the stress test. I passed the test with no signs of heart disease. Consequently, the results gave both my mother and my family some peace of mind for the time being. I wanted to be cautious and prudent for my family, but it's not something I dwell on a daily basis. I have a zest for life and a toddler-aged son that keep me both young and motivated to keep living my life.

Once my father died, I decided I needed to be closer to my mother in Lake Charles, Louisiana, during our family's grieving period. I was able to land a position at Thomas Jefferson High School in Port Arthur, Texas, about 45 minutes away from Lake Charles. I soon learned that being a high school coach in Texas is a special thing. Parents and fans put the high school coaches on a pedestal of respect. Coaching stipends are very generous, athletic equipment and facilities are first class, coaches' classroom teaching loads are reduced, and no outside fund-raising is required. Texas is also a football-driven state. Were I primarily a football coach first, I would have never left Texas. But baseball is the game I love, and I knew I couldn't stay.

A long-standing but unrealized dream of mine was to coach baseball in the state of Florida. Throughout my coaching career, I had applied for baseball positions in Florida only to be offered assistant coaching positions. I always declined those jobs because I felt as a double amputee it might be difficult for me to become a head coach again if I stepped down to an assistant coach position. All my baseball coaching experience, other than my graduate assistant year at Henderson State, has been as a head coach.

After one year at Thomas Jefferson, I was offered the position of head baseball coach at Lake Howell High School, a 6A school in Winter Park, Florida, an Orlando suburb. It had taken ten long years since my start in Campbellsville, but I had successfully worked my way back up from the lowest ranks of high school athletics to the highest high school classification, 6A, in my dream state of Florida.

As I embarked on my new challenge in sunny Florida, I carried with me a tremendous sense of satisfaction and accomplishment. It was a time for excitement and optimism. Little did I know that perhaps the greatest challenge of my life was just around the corner.

CHAPTER 8

SIERRA'S STORY

The phone call on June 26, 2000, is one I will never forget. The nurse on the other end of the line told me Susan's water had broken and she was in labor. My baby girl Sierra was on the way, which should have been a moment of joy. The problem was that her due date wasn't until September. I rushed to the hospital in Winter Park, Florida with my head swirling. What happened next would be the most difficult challenge of my life.

I was already a father at the time, which was a rather miraculous turn of events. Over the years, Susan and I had often discussed starting our own family but, after repeated difficulties, doctors told us we would never have children. By 1997 many of our friends and family members started encouraging us to try a fertility clinic.

"No, if God wants us to have children, we will," I would always respond. "And if He doesn't, we won't and we'll be fine with that." God honored that public statement of faith, and on September 30, 1998, Jordan, our first healthy baby boy was born – after 14 years of marriage.

I had come to Florida in 1997 to take over the head baseball coach position at Lake Howell High School in Winter Park. There must have been something in that Florida water, because a year after Jordan was born, Susan was pregnant again with Sierra. We were so excited to have another member of our budding family on the way so soon. We just never expected it to be such a trying experience.

Although Susan's due date was not until September, complications prompted doctors to order bed rest and have her admitted to the hospital on June 23 for the remainder of her pregnancy. Our doctors believed that if an infection developed they would catch it quickly because Susan would run a fever and show other signs of illness. Three days after she was admitted, on June 26, everything appeared to be going well. The doctors were optimistic that Susan would last two more months before delivery. I stopped at the hospital for my daily visit and returned home after several hours. The nurse called minutes after I arrived back home.

You need to get to the hospital ASAP. Susan's water has broken, and she's in labor right now!" she said.

From that point on everything was a blur. By the time I arrived back at the hospital, Susan had already delivered our daughter. The news the medical staff gave me was extremely troubling. Sierra, three months premature, weighed only 2.6 pounds and did not have a pulse or blood pressure. She had deformities in both legs, water on the brain and an E. coli infection in her umbilical chord. Doctors told us she had a 50/50 chance of survival. We were living every new parent's nightmare.

I didn't even get to see Sierra when I arrived. She was in such distress that the nurses and doctors whisked her away directly to the newborn intensive care unit to give her emergency care. Fortunately, they were able to stabilize her and place her in an incubator, where over the course of three months she would grow stronger and healthier.

Once her condition stabilized, we were informed that Sierra's leg deformities were caused by a condition called tibial hemomelia, not by the premature birth as we had initially suspected. We also learned that she was missing her front leg bone in both legs – all shocking news to me since two years earlier Jordan was born perfectly healthy. Doctors performed a DNA test and determined that I was carrying a defective gene and every child we have would have a 50-percent chance of similar leg deformities. I experienced an incredible amount of guilt and anguish upon learning that it was I who was responsible for my daughter's leg deformities.

Doctors had hoped that over time the water on Sierra's brain would dissipate, but after 18 months the fluid had not subsided. If nothing was done to relieve this, it could lead to mental retardation, so the solution was the addition of a shunt to drain the water on the brain.

At the same time, the doctors decided to perform an exploratory surgery on both of her legs to determine if they could be corrected without amputation. Unfortunately, the deformity was too severe and Sierra had to have a Simes amputation of both feet. She would eventually be fitted for prosthesis.

Initially, this was like a tremendous punch to the gut for me. The guilt and anguish returned, and I was again blaming myself for my daughter's problems. Later, because of my faith, I was able to see the situation in a larger context and realize that I was the best role model for Sierra to see what she can accomplish because I had already experienced what she will be facing. I knew that Susan and I would encourage her every step of the way and not allow her to use her handicap as an excuse. I knew, like me, her disabilities would be all she's ever known since birth, making it easier for her to adapt.

Susan and I believe in hindsight that the premature birth is what saved Sierra's life. My wife was not running a fever or experiencing any sort of sickness that would have indicated an infection. Yet, Sierra still had an E. coli infection in the umbilical chord. Had the pregnancy gone its normal term, the infection, undetected, might have proven fatal. Sierra is our miracle baby.

My wife displayed enormous strength through this long and difficult ordeal, and she was a source of tremendous support and comfort for me, never once blaming or harboring resentment towards me. We both relied heavily on our faith, prayer and the support of our church family to get through such a trying time.

People talk of being at the right place at the right time. I believe had we been in any of the other places I had coached previously in my career, we would have lost Sierra. Thankfully, we were in the Orlando area and had access to a superb hospital and doctor care. That was very nearly not the case.

The year before Sierra's birth, I had experienced a bitter disappointment that turned out to be a blessing in disguise. I was a finalist for the Seminole Community College head baseball position but was ultimately passed over despite having a solid interview and previous college coaching experience. The position would have meant a substantial pay cut and a downgrade in health insurance coverage, but I wanted badly to coach in the college ranks again. My salary and insurance coverage was considerably better with my high school position at Lake Howell.

We didn't know what the future held, but God did. He had protected us financially for the situation we would be facing a year later. It was an important life lesson for me – that sometimes what seems to be a challenge or a disappointment is actually for the best. Sometimes it just takes a little faith.

***

Today, Sierra is an active and happy 11-year-old little girl who is rarely, if ever, held back by her disability. In fact, it has perhaps been more of a challenge for me to overcome than her.

One of the toughest moments came when she was about 18 months old. Up until that point, there was hope that through surgery we could prevent amputation. Upon further investigation, the doctors found her situation to be worse than they initially suspected, and they recommended amputation of both ankles. That's when it hit me the hardest and when my guilt was at its worst. Thankfully, Sierra never shared that sentiment. I realized quickly that I could beat myself up for something I could not change, but kids are more adaptive and forgiving than adults. Sierra has never blamed me for her condition.

Over time I took comfort in the fact that I know I am the best role model for her because I have overcome the same type of obstacles she must overcome. When she complains that her legs hurt, I know exactly what she's talking about. When people doubt her, I can remind her that she should not put limits on what she can accomplish.

Knowing that she would still almost certainly face challenges due to her disability, I took the "Vinces are tough" philosophy that has served me so well, and I've passed it on to her. She immediately took it to heart. For example, since a very young age, whenever she fell she would always immediately say "I'm OK, I'm OK" before anyone could take one step toward her. She wanted to pick herself up and she always did.

Sierra has never used crutches. Very early on, she naturally adapted to her prosthesis and wanted to walk right away. In no time she could also walk or run upright on her nubs without a prosthesis. She loves to swim. At the pool she often takes off her legs and walks around on the concrete slab as if it is the most normal thing in the world. It's all she has ever known, so she has adapted to it with ease and has always been active. When she was younger, during Jordan's basketball practices, she would grab a ball and run up and down the sidelines dribbling the basketball.

Not only has Sierra never blamed me for her condition, she has developed a love for sports, particularly baseball, and has followed and come to know many of my players and teams for years. She even loves to play the game herself.

While I was serving as head baseball coach at Clearwater High School, Sierra began playing in the Little League Challenger baseball program, a league for handicapped children. It was an exciting opportunity for her because she was finally getting to participate in the sport she had always watched her father coach and her brother play.

Challenger League rules require that no matter where they hit the ball, each hitter had to circle all the bases as if hitting a home run. Sierra does it with particular gusto. Every time she comes to home plate, she has to slide. In reality, however, it's more of a flop than a slide. It's obvious that her main goal is to just get dirty. And once she's dirty, it looks like she plays baseball.

At the end of the 2010 Challenger season, Clearwater Little League hosted a weekend jamboree of games in which challenger teams from all over the state of Florida came to Clearwater to participate. At this time, the Tampa Bay Rays major league club was experiencing an unprecedented level of success in their franchise's history. Sierra and I attended numerous games together and often watched other games on television. Much to Sierra's delight, the Rays partnered with the challenger league and sent pitcher Grant Balfour and the Ray's mascot to participate in the jamboree activities. Balfour pitched to the challenger players and helped present the players their awards. Balfour graciously had his picture taken with Sierra. Later when I mailed him a copy of the picture for him to autograph, he kindly did so. It was refreshing to see that he would take time out of his hectic schedule to spend with a baseball league for handicapped children.

Sierra continues to play baseball but has now expanded into basketball and swimming at the Special Olympics. In October 2011 Sierra participated in the Louisiana State Special Olympic swim meet, where she placed first in the 25-meter event and second in the 50-meter event.

All of these sports opportunities are helping her develop positive self esteem, a strong sense of achievement, and continue to build into her life the mantra of "Vinces are tough."

There is a two year age difference between Jordan and Sierra. In the elementary grades it was uncanny to hear teachers relay stories of how protective Jordan was of Sierra. During recess, for example, kids are running and playing all over the playground as kids will do. You wouldn't think a boy Jordan's age (third grade at time) would be paying attention, but every time Sierra would fall at recess, Jordan would run to her and make sure she was OK. This was his natural instinct, not something he was told or had to be told to do.

As these siblings approach their teenage years, Sierra often complains about how annoying her brother is. She doesn't realize that, as aggravating as he may be to her sometimes outwardly, he does keep an eye out for her well-being even when she isn't aware he's doing so.

Jordan had an interest in baseball and basketball early on. This was not surprising because he always saw his dad coaching and was spending a lot of time around ball fields and gyms. Even if I weren't coaching a team in season, I was usually working the school's other athletic events in the ticket booth or running the score boards.

Jordan continues to grow and has gravitated more and more into basketball. At age 13, he is 6 feet tall and wearing a size 13 shoe. It looks as though he may grow to 6'4 or 6'5 hopefully. He now plays basketball year around on travel ball teams, recreation league teams, and school teams. He attends basketball camps in the summer. Time will tell if he continues to develop and improve his athletic skills, but he's certainly on the right track.

As Sierra's parents, we are so proud of her willingness to always try and not use her handicap as an excuse. And we are so proud of Jordan for his caring attitude. Children teach us some important lessons along the way, too.

SIERRA
AS **UPWARD BASKETBALL**
CHEERLEADER

JORDAN

CHAPTER 9

THE FLORIDA YEARS

The second I walked through that conference room door, a sense of impending doom came over me. It was 1998 and the end of my first year of coaching at Lake Howell High School, a 6A school in Winter Park. We had just wrapped up one of the school's most successful baseball seasons ever. Unfortunately, three unhappy parents of players I coached had organized a public meeting to discuss my future as head baseball coach.

When I arrived for the meeting, I was both surprised and concerned to see not only the three disgruntled families, the athletic director and principal, but also a school board member, a state legislator, as well as nearly all of the other parents from that year's team.

I was as nervous as could be. I had not expected all the other families to attend. I couldn't help but wonder if they were all there to support the three disgruntled families and help send me packing. As I sat quietly waiting for this group to determine my fate, my thoughts went back to a year earlier when I arrived in the Orlando area to take over as head baseball coach at Lake Howell.

At the time of my arrival, Lake Howell was a 30-year-old school, but the baseball program had only made the playoffs once during that span. The team was coming off an 8-19 season. There would be several players returning from that team. At first glance, a casual observer could be forgiven for thinking that having many players returning from a losing squad would be a negative. I would not accept that as an excuse.

Every place I have ever coached I put my heart and soul into the program. Every step of my coaching journey I had the task of rebuilding a downtrodden program, with the exception of my first job. My entire career I just had a knack for being able to turn programs around that weren't experiencing much success prior to my arrival. I believe my success in this way can be attributed to four steps I took at every program.

First of all, I always brought an organized, well-structured and well-disciplined program to each school. I made my baseball players lift weights long before it was trendy or commonplace. In the early days of my coaching career, I took some criticism for having my players lift weights, even though we did strength training that was tailored to the game of baseball. My philosophy was that getting physically stronger would never hurt a player. Today, every level of baseball has some type of strength training regimen. I was just a little ahead of my time.

Secondly, I always installed a rigorous conditioning and agility program. I would not allow a player to play in a game until he was able to run a mile in 6:30 or less. It was a requirement that was attainable by every player as long as they were willing to work. I had routines to help the players achieve that goal, even if they began out of shape. In fact, in 29 years of coaching I never had a player not make his time eventually.

I came to realize that it was more of a mental than physical challenge when pushing players beyond their comfort zone. The sense of achievement, accomplishment and satisfaction each player would get from achieving a goal that he perhaps thought out of reach was immeasurable. It also helped my players buy into my overall system because I helped them accomplish a goal. They realized we were then better prepared to tackle the season and achieve more goals that we set for our team.

Thirdly, because of the negativity that surrounds a program when it's not having much success, I would always bring in new uniforms and hat designs to infuse some excitement into the program. My aim was to change the perception of the program entirely. I believed that if the players felt good about themselves, the positive self-esteem would help them perform better on the field. I also forced the players to be responsible for the appearance of the playing facility. For example, I would always tell my infielders that if they had a bad hop on a ground ball, it was their fault because they hadn't manicured the playing surface well enough. These small philosophical changes went a long way in helping me change losing climates into positive and winning atmospheres.

Fourthly, I would always plan an overnight trip for the team, usually during our school's spring break. The spring break trips enabled us to bond more as a team because we shared hotel rooms, bus rides and meals together. It helped my teams develop a cohesiveness and close-knit family atmosphere that translated into positive results on and off the field.

All of these strategies together would make the program more attractive and appealing. In turn, our participation in the program increased and eventually we would see more and more success on the playing field. Finally, once we started having more success on the playing field, I would start heavily marketing my players to pro scouts and college coaches. Over my career I had five players selected in the major league draft and more than thirty receive baseball scholarships.

At Lake Howell, I implemented my standard 4-step turnaround program – with one addition: I established a fall ball AAU team. Not only would my team be conditioning and doing weight training, but in this AAU program they would be practicing and playing games. The beauty of this is that Central Florida weather is conducive to playing year round and the fall ball league lasted right up to Thanksgiving break.

By the time the spring season came around, our team had been together for six months – something they had never experienced prior to my arrival. This extra experience helped propel us to a 5-1 start early in the season. Our only loss came at the hands of 6A state runner-up Apopka (featuring future major league pitcher Zach Greinke) by a narrow margin of 1 to 0. This successful start to the season provided a tremendous confidence boost to our players and coaches. It also attracted positive media attention and recognition to a program that hadn't been experiencing any notice in recent years. With basically the same players, we went from 8-19 to a respectable 19-8.

But not everyone was happy.

It turned out that my demanding regimen of fall ball, strength training, conditioning and holding players accountable by imposing consequences when they were absent from these activities spawned three disgruntled players and their families. These three families organized what I deemed the "Fire Coach Vince" meeting. They complained to the athletic director, the principal, and the school board and demanded a public meeting to air their grievances. I certainly was shocked by this, especially after having just turned the program around from its losing ways. It was even more frustrating because the knock on the previous coach was that he wasn't doing enough to build the program, according to many of the parents. Now the knock on me was that I was doing too much.

It didn't take long, however, for me to see that my job was safe. Sixteen other parents had learned about this meeting and, although they weren't invited by the disgruntled parents, they showed up to voice their support for me and the program I had implemented. This certainly caught the group of disgruntled parents off-guard. In the eyes of the athletic director and the principal, this overwhelming show of support on my behalf was impressive. I was retained and continued as the Lake Howell baseball coach.

Any high school coach will tell you that you don't find too many administrators today with the backbone to withstand pressure from disgruntled parents. I'm eternally thankful that on that particular day my athletic director, Mike Bouch, and my principal, Don Smith, bravely stood their ground and that the 16 other players' parents cared enough to take a stand on my behalf. There's an old quote, "All it takes for evil to triumph is for good men to do nothing." Thankfully for me, a few good men and women rallied to my support.

I would like to be able to say that everything went smoothly after that, but it didn't. That first team at Lake Howell graduated numerous players, and those few disgruntled players transferred to other schools. That next team of mostly freshmen and sophomores finished with a won-loss record of 1-26 and lost 15 one-run games. I continued to encourage those players who

LAKE HOWELL HAWKS DISTRICT CHAMPIONS

went through such a tough experience, continually telling them that "those that remain will become champions." That statement became reality as each of the next four years we fought our way to the district championship game, winning it twice and advancing to the state playoffs all four years – a feat that had only been accomplished once prior to my arrival. I stayed at Lake Howell for seven years, the longest of any place in my career. It was a tremendous experience.

My next stop in Florida would be Monarch High School in Coconut Creek in South Florida near Fort Lauderdale. Monarch was a brand new school in its second year of existence when I arrived. The athletic director, Ollie Pottmeyer, had been both a head college football and head college baseball coach. An assistant

MONARCH KNIGHTS WITH FRANK VIOLA—
WORLD SERIES MVP MINNESOTA TWINS, '87;
CY YOUNG, AWARD WINNER '88

principal, Mr. Hendricks, had pitched in the major leagues with the Cleveland Indians in the 60s. I was excited to get this coaching opportunity because the baseball talent pool in south Florida is tremendous and the school was only 30 minutes from the Florida Marlins stadium.

One of the most memorable moments from my time at Monarch was our spring break trip to Las Vegas to participate in the Durango High School tourney. We toured the Hoover Dam, visited the Grand Canyon, attended a Los Angeles Dodgers Triple A minor league game, walked the Vegas strip and played four baseball games. It was a trip of a lifetime, and we gave every player a highlight DVD of that trip and that season. I also gained another lifelong friend in assistant coach Jim Dingus.

During my time at Monarch, unfortunately a horrific tragedy occurred. One fall day of my second year at Monarch, my team and I were working a fundraiser at the NHL Florida Panthers hockey game. Meanwhile, back at the school, the junior varsity football team was hosting a game. Midway through the third quarter of the football game, our athletic director noticed a bolt of lightning approximately three miles away. Although it wasn't raining and really wasn't very cloudy, Coach Pottmeyer immediately stopped the game and began trying to evacuate the field.

Florida leads the nation not only in lightning strikes but also in deaths caused by lightning, so administrators and coaches are usually cautious when thunderstorms approach. Coach Pottmeyer, not taking any risks, was frantically trying to clear the area when a bolt of lightning struck the football field. The strike threw Coach Pottmeyer completely out of his golf cart, knocked 50 spectators to the ground, and tragically struck a football player in the chest between the shoulder pads, killing him instantly. Three others sustained serious injuries and were hospitalized for several days.

It is impossible to overstate the emotional toll this tragedy took on our school. Our baseball field was positioned right next to the football field, and on any given day the baseball team would have been right there, too, holding practice. We just happened to be away at the fundraiser.

For months after this tragedy, students would become very frightened if clouds darkened or rain threatened. As coaches, we began immediately ending practices and games at the hint of a storm. Prior to this tragedy occurring, I would just hold kids in the dugouts and wait for the storm to pass. That would no longer be the case. It just wasn't worth the risk.

Our administration had done and continued to do everything right in the handling of the situation, and its aftermath and certainly was not at fault. It was simply an act of God. Still, the impact was swift and severe. At the end of this particular school year, our principal, Kathy Collins resigned. When she resigned, our athletic director, Coach Pottmeyer, retired. I had developed an extremely close relationship with both of these people.

Soon after their resignations, I, too, would resign and move on to another opportunity.

***

What would prove to be my final coaching stop was Clearwater High School about 20 miles west of Tampa. The city of Clearwater is the spring training home of the Philadelphia Phillies and also home to the Phillies Class A minor league team, the Clearwater Threshers. It's a great baseball town with a long history. Unlike Monarch High School, which existed for only two years when I arrived, Clearwater High School was more than a hundred years old. Some famous Clearwater alumni include Howard Johnson of the '86 World Champion New York Mets, Auburn University Head Football Coach Gene Chizik, and NASA astronaut Nicole Passonno Stott. I felt very honored and blessed to have an opportunity to coach at the school.

I inherited some tremendously talented players and an active and supportive booster club. Several players of mine are currently playing baseball in college. Craig Goodman is a senior right-handed pitcher at Tusculum College in Tennessee (senior 2012). Tim Younger is a senior second baseman at East Carolina University. Kraig Richmond is a sophomore right-handed pitcher at Tallahassee Community College. Sean O'Brien is a sophomore outfielder at Florida State (in 2012).

CRAIG GOODMAN

2008

CLEARWATER TORNADOES 2008

PICTURE TAKEN AT BRIGHTHOUSE STADIUM,
SPRING TRAINING HOME OF PHILADELPHIA PHILLIES

SEAN O'BRIEN

While I was at Clearwater High School, our program had a great relationship with the Phillies and the Threshers. During spring training, our booster parents were allowed to work a concession trailer grilling hot dogs, hamburgers and selling drinks during the first two or three weeks of spring training practices. The fact that the Phillies were in the World Series two of the three years I was at Clearwater certainly enhanced the crowds attending spring training and thereby increased the funds we were able to raise.

The Threshers allowed us opportunities to work some of their home game concessions, and the Phillies major league club was also gracious enough to allow us to play an annual Red/Gray game in the major league stadium and put our players' pictures up on the jumbotron scoreboard. It was such a thrill for our team.

SEMINOLE HIGH SCHOOL VS. CLEARWATER HIGH SCHOOL, COACH GREG OLSON #25

The Phillies also donated 50 wood bats to my baseball program each fall for our use in the fall ball wood bat league.

I would like to thank the Philadelphia Phillies and Clearwater Threshers for their generosity toward Clearwater during my stint as their head coach. My principal Keith Mastorides and Athletic Director Kathy Biddle were also tremendously supportive of both me personally and my baseball program. They helped make my final three years in coaching a very pleasurable and memorable experience.

But it wasn't meant to last forever. In the middle of my third year at Clearwater, my wife and I got some surprising news. She was pregnant, which meant at age 50 I would become a father again. Our son Hunter was born March 11, 2010, and his birth changed everything for my family. But I take with me so many blessed memories of good people.

***

Hello Coach Vince-

Debbie and I have just returned from a very memorable baseball weekend in North Carolina. I'm writing to both share the events AND thank you for your role in the development of our son, Tim.

In short, Tim was awarded the honor of wearing jersey number 23 for his senior year of baseball at East Carolina University. The following links best explain the honor and its importance to the community of Greenville, NC as it represents a most-loved baseball coach, Keith Leclair, who died of Lou Gehrig's disease in 2006.

TV report (WNCT)
http://www2.wnct.com/news/2012/jan/28/ecu-baseball-player-receives-23-leclairs-honor-ar-1866308/

ECU Website
http://www.ecupirates.com/sports/m-basebl/spec-rel/012812aaa.html

As parents, there are times when we have to give our sons and daughters over to others in their life journeys. We recognize that what you have done with Tim and what you continue to do with others is extremely important. Debbie and I also want you to know how much we appreciate it. We will always remember your tireless effort and continued support of the young men you coached at Clearwater High School. Your example and leadership is very much a part of who Tim is and what he is about.

May God continue to bless you and yours.

Sincerely,

Mark and Debbie Younger

(with permission)

TIM YOUNGER, INFIELDER
ST. PETERSBURG CC
EAST CAROLINA UNIVERSITY
(SENIOR, 2012)

CHAPTER 10

LIFE'S LESSONS THROUGH SPORTS

Throughout my coaching career I always adopted a slogan or a theme for each season and used that theme as a motivational tool throughout the year. These themes extended always beyond the game itself and helped reinforce important life lessons that I tried to teach through athletics. Some of these slogans are familiar and popular sayings, but they proved effective when applied the correct way over the course of a season.

One such slogan was "Be the Hammer Not the Nail." Most baseball programs where I've coached were losing before I arrived, so the bulk of my career was spent rebuilding downtrodden programs. In this theme, the metaphorical nail is always being beaten by the hammer, just as the programs I took over were on the receiving end of numerous losses. Losing can be habit-forming, just as winning can be contagious. When the program has been down for an extended period of time, the players often begin to accept losing or at least approach the game expecting to lose.

I used this theme to encourage everyone around the team to quit accepting losing as normal and to change the culture of negative expectations. I told my players that they should be the team that delivers the beating (the hammer) instead of being the team that receives the beating (the nail). I emphasized that this was a philosophy or attitude that one should carry with them daily.

To transform this abstract concept into something concrete for the players to see, I built a board with the names of our district opponents written on a series of nails. Our school mascot was the one holding the hammer. Some of those schools still beat us, but we were more competitive because of our change in attitude. I have found that a winning attitude goes a long way towards success on and off the field. I've also found that confidence and self-esteem in sports transfers to other parts of life.

Another theme I often used was "What's right is not always what's popular. What's popular is not always what's right. But always do what's right."

It's no secret that teenagers often fall prey to peer pressure. They're often tempted by their peers to smoke, drink, do drugs, have sex. In the moment, some simply give in because everyone around them at that time is doing it. They often feel, if they were to resist the pressure at that moment, they would become less popular (and perhaps they would with that particular crowd). But this theme encouraged my kids to do the right thing – even at the risk of losing popularity. I always told them to be a leader rather than a follower and stand up for what is right, even it isn't very popular.

In fact, "Do what's right" was our most important team policy. I would drive this sort of disciplined approach home through a series of small but important team rules. For example, we always wore our hats straight, not crooked, tucked our shirts in and cleaned up after ourselves at restaurants. When we visited a fast food restaurant as a team, we took off our hats inside and didn't leave until every player had cleaned up his table. I told my players that when we go to a fast food restaurant, we could present the only image the workers see of our school, so they may judge our entire school on how we act. Plenty of people have asked me what does that have to do with winning baseball games? Well, I don't know for sure, but I do know it was the right thing to do. These were life lessons for my teams and helped create an atmosphere of discipline and responsibility that translated into a better team on the field.

I've often heard stories about college and high school teams trashing hotel rooms on road trips. Many businesses are reluctant to house sports teams because of those horror stories. But on more than one occasion I received a letter from the hotel manager bragging about how well mannered my kids were in the hotel. The legendary LSU baseball coach Skip Bertman used to say you're representing God, your family and your school, in that order, and I wholeheartedly agree.

Another successful theme that I used over and over again is "Hold the Rope," which is a slogan designed to encourage teamwork. The nature of the game of baseball makes supporting your teammates in down times an essential component of good team chemistry. When you think about it, the game of baseball is most times a game of failure. A hitter with a .300 batting average has failed 7 out of 10 times, yet is recognized as being quite successful. Even the multi-million dollar players at the major league level have bad days or weeks when their pitching, fielding, throwing or hitting skills are off.

My philosophy is that when some players are having a bad game, the other players have to step up their game and take up the slack for the team to be able to win. I told my players not to use a bad day by another player as an excuse to lose, but to instead have the attitude of "just win anyway." That's where the concept of "hold the rope" comes in.

I would tell my players to imagine that if they were dangling from a cliff with their lives at stake, who would they want holding the rope? It would certainly be someone they trusted that no matter the cost – whether it was pain, soreness, fatigue, hunger, thirst – would not let go of that rope. I would emphasize that our team needed to reach a point with our team chemistry that every player on that roster would be that kind of supportive and strong guy for his teammate. If an umpire's call went against us, we said "hold the rope." If a player made an error or struck out with the bases loaded, we responded with "hold the rope" and thought about how we could win. This theme is a positive way to avoid making excuses while also encouraging everyone to focus on what they can do to help overcome the adversity the team is facing.

One of my favorite slogans was "the only place success comes before work is in the dictionary!" So many people today are looking for easy street. To that I say, where the heck is easy street? Too many people want the instant fix, the least challenging road to success or prosperity, and many expect it to be handed to them on a silver platter. Many of these types of folks don't want to attain their success the old fashioned way and consequently never develop a work ethic to help them achieve greatness.

I've learned time and time again that on the road to excellence there are no shortcuts. Many people have the will to win, but few have the will to prepare to win. Success looks easy to those who weren't around when it was being earned. Once one gives extraordinary efforts to attain success, that success is much more gratifying and less likely to be taken for granted. Nothing of real value comes easily or through shortcuts.

One of my Lake Howell High School teams went 1-26, but then the same players won the district championship the very next year. I know that having been through the adversity the prior season, my players gained a greater appreciation for the championship once it was attained. They absolutely did not take it for granted. The sense of satisfaction was so great because they were able to look back on all the effort they put into weight lifting, conditioning and fall ball. They understood that the hard work is what led them to the prize.

I feel strongly that approach and attitude are the foundations on which success is built. This is a fact that I've observed both as a coach on the field and as I examine my own life. The keys to my own success were not natural ability or lucky breaks, but rather the result of hard work and persistence. I often boil my formula for life success down to three key elements: determination, dedication and desire.

Doctors told my parents I'd never walk without crutches, but my parents simply wouldn't allow the word "can't" in my vocabulary. It was always "try." They never let me use my handicap as an excuse. When I was eight years old, I became a Christian and discovered two scripture verses that I patterned the rest of my life around. The first was Romans 8:28, which promises that "All things work together for the good of those who love God and are called according to His purpose." The second was Philippians 4:13, which says: "I can do all things through Christ which strengthens me."

Once I read these two verses, I could no longer feel sorry for myself. I realized I needed to get over the fact that I was handicapped and quit using it as an excuse for not achieving. This is when I first became **determined** to achieve. I took swimming lessons at the YMCA and learned to swim. I put the crutches down, and I never looked back. By the time I got to college, I was determined I would build a career coaching baseball and overcome all obstacles.

That brings me to **dedication**. Having never played the game, I knew I wouldn't have instant name credibility with athletic directors or players. I had to overcome that by being very knowledgeable of the sport. I went to coaches clinics all over the U.S., read books on baseball coaching and picked the brains of legendary coaches Skip Bertman, Ron Polk, Augie Garrido and Gary Ward. I also attended junior college games, college games and professional games looking for drills, techniques and strategies that I could apply. I put in the work in order to achieve my success.

The final element is **desire.** I have always had a passion for the game of baseball, and I put my heart and soul into my work. And what I got out was immensely rewarding. While I'm proud of my personal achievements, the ones that mean the most to me are those that helped kids reach their potential. Having five players get drafted by major league teams, having more than thirty players receive scholarships to play in college, and the relationships I developed with these players are what mean the most to me. I still have former players contact me to this day. Knowing I had a positive influence on their lives is the most satisfying achievement.

If you believe in yourself, set high goals, be unwavering in your effort to make it happen despite all the odds and obstacles you face, you can succeed in life. It just takes the right winning attitude and a little determination, dedication and desire.

CHAPTER 11

RETIREMENT REFLECTIONS

As the 2009-2010 school year at Clearwater High School in Florida approached, I was satisfied with where I was in my career and life. I was a successful baseball coach at a quality school that supported its athletic programs in a great part of the country. I thought I had unfinished business in baseball, so I assumed I would coach for five more years, then retire.

I figured it would likely take two more years for me to reach the milestone 500th career win, something I really wanted to attain. Five more years as a coach would put my age at 55 and my career experience at 34 years, the uniform number I wore my entire career. I thought it would make for a storybook ending.

However, God had other plans. Our third child, Hunter, was born March 11, 2010. I was 50 and my wife was 47. The first thought that entered my mind when I realized my wife was pregnant was that I would be 70 years old when this baby is in college. His pending arrival certainly forced me to go back to the drawing board to figure out what I thought was a reasonable and prudent five-year plan. Suddenly, achieving 500 career victories didn't seem so important.

And as the birth of Hunter approached, my mother began putting a bug in my ear. "It's time to come home," she said. By "home" she meant back to Louisiana, since more than two decades of my coaching career were spent outside the bayou state. She lived in a rural area 25 miles north of Lake Charles, Louisiana, on four-and-a-half acres of land. To further entice me to move home, she offered us an acre of land and promised to be regularly available to help keep the baby.

Those factors certainly played into our decision, but ultimately it was something else that brought me back to Louisiana. Although I was the oldest child in my family, both my younger brother and younger sister now had adult children who were raised around "granny," as they called my mother. Because my coaching career carried me hundreds of miles away, my children were not experiencing their childhoods around their grandmother. But with Jordan and Sierra still only 11 and 9 respectively – and now with newborn Hunter, it was not too late for my children to experience a close relationship with their grandmother.

Add to that the fact that cost of daycare in Florida for Hunter would have exceeded my wife's monthly income as a teacher's aide, and the correct choice came into focus. After much thought and prayer, I made the difficult decision to retire in July of 2010. I was leaving the world of baseball after 29 years of teaching and coaching and 470 career wins.

I wasn't sure how I was going to handle not coaching anymore, no longer being part of competitive sports and not working with young men on and off the field. At the time I retired, I still felt in my heart that my passion for baseball was still prevalent, although my passion for the classroom had certainly waned. Baseball had consumed my life year-round for nearly three decades, which is why I honestly thought life without baseball was going to be a difficult transition to make.

To my surprise, I did not miss it as much as I thought I would have. I still stay around baseball by giving private lessons and attending college and high school games. The game has always been in my blood and will always be a part of my life, so I could never leave it completely behind. But it is no longer my primary focus, and I have found peace with this change in my life.

The move back to Louisiana and more specifically to an area so far from a major city has been a positive one for my family, although admittedly it has been a definite lifestyle change. We were accustomed to living five minutes from anything we needed: the bank, the post office, the grocery store, a gas station, restaurants. Now we are 17 miles from all those places. The extra cost of gasoline required for those extra drives was an expense that we did not anticipate and has taken time to get used to. However, my kids quickly took to the wide open spaces, love playing on the four-and-a-half acres of land and relish the opportunity to interact with their granny on a daily basis.

As for me, I settled into my new role as a stay-at-home Dad with Hunter. Retirement has also afforded me time and opportunity to get involved with community service. I am currently the vice president of the Moss Bluff Lions Club and also serve as the league administrator for the Moss Bluff Recreational Basketball League. I am an active member of the Gideons International, which is a group of men who raise funds and distribute Bibles to hotels, hospitals, nursing homes, prisons and public schools.

As I reflect on my three-decade coaching career, I can't help but be proud of and pleased with what I accomplished. I am reminded of former major league player Sammy Sosa's quote: "Baseball has been very, very good to me." That statement certainly embodies my feelings today.

In addition to the on-field success, baseball afforded me opportunities to have traveled to 43 of the 50 states and 8 foreign countries. Several times I traveled overseas with baseball players from all over the nation to play baseball against teams from other countries, provide baseball clinics, sightsee and experience foreign cultures.

Organizations such as Athletes in Action, Coast to Coast Baseball, USAAI, and Tourney Sport provided airfare, housing and two meals a day for me to travel and coach baseball teams. Through these organizations, I had the opportunity to coach baseball in Holland, Spain, Czech Republic, Sweden, Australia, Italy, Puerto Rico four times, Curacao, and Hawaii. I probably would have never visited any of these places had it not been for baseball.

I think back with fond memories of some of the legendary major league managers and players I was able to meet through my coaching career. I met men like Sparky Anderson, Tommy Lasorda, Tony Larussa, Johnny Bench, Wade Boggs, Paul Molitor, David Eckstein and Matt Lawton. I think of the great players I coached against in high school who are now in the major leagues: Eric Hosmer, Felipe Lopez, Billy Butler, Zack Greinke, Rickie Weeks, Prince Fielder and Johnny Venters.

Most of all, I am thankful for the relationships I've developed with my players and fellow coaches along the way. These people enriched my life for so many years and made this baseball journey an important and unforgettable one. I hope I was able to have a positive influence and leave a lasting impression on all with whom I came in contact on and off the field.

In conclusion, I would be remiss if I didn't thank all of the principals and athletic directors that were willing to take a risk by hiring an above-knee double amputee baseball coach:

Clifton Matherne/Jim Hightower-Catholic Pointe Coupee HS

Albert Lafrance, Jr./Carl Ward   Port Sulphur HS

Dr. Clyde Berry/Dr. Michael O'Quinn-Henderson State Univ.

Don Bishop   Campbellsville University

James Charles/Andy Breaux   Ellender HS

Buddy Singleton   Harrison Central HS

Larry Walker   Thomas Jefferson HS

Don Smith/Mike Bouch   Lake Howell HS

Kathy Collins/Ollie Pottmeyer   Monarch HS

Gary Seale/Jim Pierce   Campbell County HS

Keith Mastorides/Kathy Biddle   Clearwater HS

Finally, when life throws you curves, remember Joshua 10:25: "Do not be afraid or discouraged. Be strong and courageous, for the Lord will do this to all the enemies you fight."

We all face battles of different kinds today. From financial problems, health problems, spiritual struggles to emotional instability and crumbling relationships—these are all real issues people face each and every day. It's easy to get discouraged when facing all that life throws at us. It is often easy to feel like the underdog. Sometimes it can appear there's no end in sight, no rest from the challenges we face. The battles we have to fight can often seem too great, the odds too overwhelming, the enemies too strong. Defeat can seem inevitable.

But if there is a message I hope people take from my own story: it's to not give up. Don't ever give up!

God is bigger than any obstacle we face. When we move out of the way, stop trying to figure things out on our own, and we trust God to intercede and fight our battles for us, we are inviting HIM to show us just how really big HE is. Refocus your discouragement and doubt into strength and courage and trust in God for the outcome. Joshua 10:25 is not a premise, it's a promise!

Forever in HIS Grip.

JORDAN, SIERRA, AND HUNTER

— MORE MEMORIES —

WADE BOGGS MLB HALL OF FAME 2005

**GLENN SCOTT
ASSISTANT COACH,
LAKE HOWELL**

**BCAA All-Star Baseball Classic
North All-Stars
2006**

**Campbell County High School, TN
Forefront: Blake Potter
Background: Ben Aiken (Graduated from Air Force
Academy)**

**DAVID WITH TONY LARUSSA, WORLD SERIES
CHAMPION ST. LOUIS CARDINALS MANAGER**

To Contact Coach Vince

David Vince
736 Texas Eastern Road
Ragley, Louisiana 70657

E-mail: vncfam5@aol.com
Cell phone: 337-842-8754

www.davidvince.com

About Jeremy M. Harper, Co-author

Jeremy Harper is a freelance writer and designer based in Baton Rouge, Louisiana. He has written about politics, hurricanes and sports in Louisiana over a decade for daily newspapers and online publications across the state.

— TO ORDER —

When Life Throws You Curves, Keep Swinging
A Memoir by Coach David Vince
With Jeremy M. Harper

You may order on David Vince's website
www.davidvince.com
or E-mail at vncfam5@aol.com

or from
LangMarc Publishing
www.langmarc.com
Bookstores: Call LangMarc at 1-800-864-1648

Please send me _____ copies of
When Life Throws You Curves, Keep Swinging
at $19.95 + $3 shipping

Your name _____

Street Address _____

City, State, Zip _____

Phone no. _____

*Check enclosed for $*_____
      or
Credit Card Number _____

_____

Expiration date: _____

CPSIA information can be obtained at www.ICGtesting.com
Printed in the USA
BVOW00s1857300114

343372BV00008B/251/P

9 781880 292457